Edward de Bone

By the same author

Atlas of Management Thinking
Children Solve Problems
Conflicts: A Better Way to Solve Them
Future Positive
Lateral Thinking
Lateral Thinking for Management
Letters to Thinkers
Opportunities
PO: Beyond Yes and No
Practical Thinking
Six Thinking Hats
Teach Your Child how to Think
Teaching Thinking
The Five-Day Course in Thinking
The Happiness Purpose
The Mechanism of Mind
Wordpower
I am Right – You are Wrong
Edward de Bono's Masterthinker's Handbook
Handbook for the Positive Revolution
Serious Creativity
Surpetition
Six Action Shoes

WATER LOGIC

Edward de Bono

VIKING

VIKING

Published by the Penguin Group
Penguin Books Ltd, 27 Wrights Lane, London W8 5TZ, England
Penguin Books USA Inc., 375 Hudson Street, New York, New York 10014, USA
Penguin Books Australia Ltd, Ringwood, Victoria, Australia
Penguin Books Canada Ltd, 10 Alcorn Avenue, Toronto, Ontario, Canada M4V 3B2
Penguin Books (NZ) Ltd, 182–190 Wairau Road, Auckland 10, New Zealand

Penguin Books Ltd, Registered Offices: Harmondsworth, Middlesex, England

First published 1993
1 3 5 7 9 10 8 6 4 2
First edition

Copyright © McQuaig Group Inc., 1993

The moral right of the author has been asserted

Typeset by Datix International, Bungay, Suffolk
Printed in England by Clays Ltd, St Ives plc

A CIP catalogue record for this book is available from the British Library

ISBN 0–670–851256

FOREWORD

Johnny was a young boy who lived in Australia. One day his friends offered him a choice between a one dollar coin and a two dollar coin. In Australia the one dollar coin is considerably larger than the two dollar coin. Johnny took the one dollar coin. His friends giggled and laughed and reckoned Johnny very stupid because he did not yet know that the smaller coin was worth twice as much as the bigger coin. Whenever they wanted to demonstrate Johnny's stupidity they would repeat the exercise. Johnny never seemed to learn.

One day a bystander felt sorry for Johnny and beckoning him over, the bystander explained that the smaller coin was actually worth twice as much as the larger coin.

Johnny listened politely, then he said: 'Yes, I do know that. But how many times would they have offered me the coins if I had taken the two dollar coin the first time?'

A computer which has been programmed to select value would have had to choose the two dollar coin the first time around. It was Johnny's human 'perception' that allowed him to take a different and longer-term view: the possibility of repeat business, the possibility of several more one dollar coins. Of course, it was a risk and the perception was very complex: how often would he see his friends? Would they go on using the same game? Would they want to go on losing one dollar coins, etc.?

There are two points about this story which are relevant to this book.

The first point is the great importance of human perception, and that is what this book is about. Perception is rather different from our traditional concept of logic.

The second point arising from the story is the difference between the thinking of Johnny and the thinking of the computer. The thinking of the computer would be based on 'is'. The computer would say to itself: 'Which of the two coins "is" the most valuable?' As a result the computer would choose the smaller, two dollar coin. The thinking of Johnny was not based on 'is' but on 'to': 'What will this lead to?' 'What will happen if I take the one dollar coin?' Traditional rock logic is based on 'is'. The logic of perception is water logic and this is based on 'to'.

The basic theme of the book is astonishingly simple. In fact it is so simple that many people will find it hard to understand. Such people feel that things ought to be complex in order to be serious. Yet most complex matters turn out to be very simple once they are understood. Because the theme is so simple I shall attempt to describe it as simply as possible. Although the basic theme is simple the effects are powerful, important and complex.

I have always been interested in practical outcomes. There are many practical processes, techniques and outcomes covered in this book. How would you like to 'see' your thinking as clearly as you might see a landscape from an aeroplane? There is a way of doing that which I shall describe. This can be of great help in understanding our perceptions and even in altering them.

I know that my books attract different sorts of readers. There are those who are genuinely interested in the long neglected subject of thinking and there are those who are only interested in practical 'hands-on' techniques. The latter type of reader may be impatient with the underlying theory, which is seen to be complex and unnecessary. I would like to be able to say to this sort of reader: 'Skip section ... and section ...' But I will not do that because thinking has suffered far too much from a string of gimmicks that have no foundation. It is very important to understand the theoretical basis in order to use the processes with real motivation. Furthermore the underlying processes are fascinating in themselves. Understanding how the brain works is a subject of great interest.

I have used no mathematical expressions in the book because it is a mistake to believe that mathematics (the behaviour of relationships and processes within a defined universe) has to be expressed in mathematical symbols which most people do not understand. Some years ago Professor Murray Gell-Mann, the California Institute of Technology professor who won a Nobel prize in physics for inventing/discovering/describing the quark, was given my book *The Mechanism of Mind* which was published in 1969. He told me that he had found it very interesting because I had 'stumbled upon processes ten years before the mathematicians had started to describe them'. These are the processes of self-organizing systems which interested him for his work on chaos.

This book is a first look at water logic and my intention has been to put forward a method for using it in a practical manner.

INTRODUCTION

This book is closely related to my previous book *I am Right – You are Wrong* (London: Viking, 1990 and Penguin 1991). In that book I set out to show that the traditional habits of Western thinking were inadequate and how our belief in their adequacy was both limiting and dangerous. These traditional habits include: the critical search for the 'truth'; argument and adversarial exploration, and all the characteristics of rock logic with its crudities and harshness. These habits of thinking were ultimately derived from the classic Greek gang of three, Socrates, Plato and Aristotle, who hijacked Western thinking. After the dogma of the Dark Ages, the rediscovery of this classical thinking was indeed a breath of fresh air and so these habits were taken up both by the Church (to provide a weapon for attacking heresy) and by the non-Church humanist thinkers to provide an escape from Church dogma. So it became the established thinking of Western civilization.

Unfortunately this thinking lacks the creative, design and constructive energies that we so badly need. Nor does this thinking take into account the huge importance of perception, beliefs and local truths. Finally this rock logic exacerbates the worst deficiencies of the human brain, which is why we have made progress in technical matters and so little in human affairs. For the first time in history we do know something, in broad terms, about how the brain works as a self-organizing information system – and this has important implications.

As I predicted the book was met with outrage that was so hysterical that it became comic and ludicrous rather than offensive. Not one of those who attacked the book ever challenged its basic themes. The attacks were in the nature of childish personal abuse or picked on very minor matters – which is always a sure indication that the reviewer is not reviewing the book but prefers to attack the author. This is a pity because it is a serious subject which needs much more attention than it gets.

It was Einstein who once said: 'Great spirits have always encountered violent opposition from mediocre minds.' It does not follow that violent opposition from mediocre minds qualifies one automatically as a great spirit but it does suggest that the violence of the opposition sometimes indicates emotions rather than value.

To redress this balance, because the subject is important, I invited three Nobel prize physicists to write forewords to the book for future editions. Those forewords put the matter into perspective. Why physicists? Because physicists spend their whole lives looking at fundamental processes and their implications.

I had intended to add a section on water logic and 'hodics' to the book. In the end the book became too long and it was obvious that the section would have to be too short to do justice to the subject. I promised I would treat the subject in a subsequent publication, and that is what this book is about.

In our tradition of thinking we have sought to get away from the vagueness and instability of perception in order to deal with such concrete matters as mathematics and logic. We have done reasonably well at this and can now get back to dealing with perception as such. Indeed we have no choice because if our perceptions are faulty then perfect processing of those faulty perceptions can only give an answer that is wrong, and sometimes dangerous. We know from experience that both sides in any war, conflict or disagreement always have 'logic' on their side. This is true: a logic that serves their particular perceptions.

So this book is about the water logic of perception.

How do perceptions come about? What is the origin and nature of perception? How do the nerve circuits in the brain form and use perceptions? How do perceptions become stable — and stable enough to become beliefs? Can we get to look at our perceptions regarding any particular matter? Can we change perceptions — and if so, where do we start?

This book does not provide all the answers but at the end of it the reader should have a good understanding of the difference between water logic and rock logic.

STRUCTURE OF THE BOOK

I start by considering the importance of perception which is the working of the inner world of the mind. This is different from the outer world which surrounds us. Traditionally we have tried to get away from perception to deal with the 'truth' of reality. It is time we looked directly at perception.

The next section introduces the notion of water logic and 'flow'. Traditional logic is rock logic and is based on 'is' and identity. Water logic is based on 'to': what does this flow to?

An analogy involving the behaviour of simple jellyfish then illustrates how 'flow' works to give stability in a self-organizing system. Different flow patterns are illustrated.

There is now a direct consideration of the 'flow behaviour' of the brain and how this gives rise to perception. The jellyfish analogy is transferred to the behaviour of nerve circuits in the brain but the principles remain the same.

A practical technique called the 'flowscape' is now introduced. This technique enables us to see the 'shape' of our perceptions. I explain how flowscapes are created.

A stream of consciousness provides the items for the 'base list' from which the flowscape is derived. The nature of this list is discussed.

There follows a consideration of flowscapes that are more complex, with comments upon these.

The next section deals with the great importance of

concepts in water logic and in perception. Concepts give us flexibility and movement in thinking. These concepts do not need to be precise and a little fuzziness is beneficial.

We may want to see how we might intervene to alter perceptions. This section is concerned with methods of intervention based on the flowscape. Although the flowscapes are concerned with the inner world of perception, we can derive from the flowscapes some strategies for dealing with the outer world.

The notion of context is central to water logic because if the context changes then the flow direction may also change. This is very different from the assumed absolutes of rock logic.

Being based on perception, flowscapes are highly personal. Nevertheless, it is possible to attempt to chart the perceptions of others. This can be done in a number of ways ranging from discussion to guessing. Even guessing can suggest usable strategies.

The flow of our attention over the outer world is strongly influenced by the perceptual patterns we have set up in the inner world. This is considered in this section as is the relationship between art and attention flows.

The practical difficulties that might be encountered in setting up flowscapes are now considered with some suggestions as to how they might be overcome.

The summary pulls together the nature of water logic
and the practical technique of the flowscape. Water logic
does not exist only as a contrast to rock logic.

Edward de Bono

Palazzo Marnisi
Malta

OUTER WORLD
INNER WORLD

The original title of this section was going to be 'Perception and Reality'. In the traditional way this would have suggested that there was reality 'somewhere out there' and then there was perception which was different from reality. But perception is just as real as anything else – in fact perception is more real for the person involved. A child's terror at a moving curtain in the night is very real. A schizophrenic's anguish at inner voices is very real. In fact, perception is the only reality for the person involved. It is not usually a shared reality and may not check with the world out there, but perception is certainly real.

For centuries Western thinking has been dominated by the analogy of Plato's cave in which a person chained so that he can only see the back of the cave, sees only the shadows projected on this surface and not the 'reality' that has caused the shadows. So philosophers have generally looked for the 'truth' that gives rise to these shadows or perceptions. It is quite true that some people, like Freud and Jung in particular, focused their attention on the shadows, but not on perception in general. This lack of interest in perception is understandable. People wanted to get away from the messiness of perception to the solidity of truth. More importantly, you cannot do much except describe perceptions unless you have some understanding of how they work. That understanding we have come to only very recently.

A Georgian manor house is set on its own in the fields. A party of people arrive for the weekend. They are all looking at the same house. One person looks at it with nostalgia for happy times spent there. Another person looks at it with envy, thinking of the sort of life style she would want. A third person looks at it with horror, remembering a harsh childhood spent in the house. A fourth person immediately assesses how much such a house would cost. The house is the same in each case and a photograph taken by each of the people would show the same house. But the inner world of perception is totally different.

In the case of the house seen differently the physical view is the same but the memory trails and emotional attachments provide the different inner world of perception. But perception could still be different even if there were no special memory trails. If each of the guests were to approach the house from a different direction they would get a different point of view. It would be the same house perceived from a different perspective. The person approaching from the front would get the classic Georgian facade. A person approaching from the side would see the original Elizabethan house on to which the facade had been tacked. The person approaching from the back might mistake the house for a farm.

Everyone knows of the classic optical illusions in which you look at a drawing on a piece of paper and what you think you see is not actually the case: lines which seem to bend but are actually straight; a shape that looks larger than another but is exactly equal. Stage magicians perform the magnificent feat of fooling all the people all the time through tricking their perceptions. We are left waiting for the event to occur while it has occurred a long time before.

It is obvious that perception is very individual and that perception may not correspond with the external world. Perception, in the first place, is the way the brain organizes the information received from the outer world via the senses. The type of organization that is possible depends entirely on the fundamental nature of the nerve circuits in the brain. This organization is then affected by the emotional state of the moment which favours some patterns at the expense of others. The short-term memory of the present context and what has gone immediately before affects perception. Computer translation of language is so difficult because what has gone before, and the context, may totally alter the meaning of the word. For example, the word 'live' is pronounced in two different ways depending on the context. Finally there are the old memories and memory trails which can both alter what we perceive and attach themselves to the perception.

One of the most striking examples of the power of perception is the phenomenon of jealousy. A man is accused of choosing to sit in a certain place in a restaurant so that he can stare at the blonde sitting opposite. In truth, he had not even noticed the blonde and was really trying to give his girlfriend the seat with the best view. A wife seems to be seeing a lot of a certain man in the course of her business. She claims it is a business relationship but her husband thinks otherwise. In jealousy there are complex interpretations of normal situations which may be totally false and yet give rise to powerful emotions, quarrels and violence. The point is that the perceptions could, just possibly, be true. The fact that they are not true does not alter the perceptions.

It is no wonder that the ancient thinkers considered it a magnificent feat to get away from this highly subjective business of perception to truths and absolutes which could be checked and which would hold for everyone.

If you were making a table you could guess the sizes of the pieces that you needed and just cut them up according to your guess. You would probably be better off if you were to measure the pieces you needed. They would then be more likely to fit together and the table legs would be the same height. Measurement is a very successful way of changing perception into something that is concrete, tangible and permanent. We take it for granted but it is a wonderful concept.

Mathematics is another method for escaping the uncertainties of perception. We translate the world into symbols and relationships. Once this is done we enter the 'game world' of mathematics with its own special universe and rules of behaviour within that universe. We play that game in a rigorous manner. Then we translate the result back into the real world. The method works very well indeed provided the mathematics is appropriate and the translation into and out of the system is valid.

The great contribution of the Greek gang of three was to set out to do the same thing with language. Words were going to have specific definitions and to be as real, concrete and objective as is measurement. Then there was going to be a rigorous game with rules which would tell us how to put words together and how to reason. This game was largely based on identity: this thing 'is' or 'is not' something else. The principle of contradiction held that something could not 'be' and 'not be' something at the same time. From this basis we developed our systems of language, logic, argument, critical thinking and all the other habits which we use all the time.

The result was that we seemed able to make judgements (which the human brain loves) and to arrive at truths and certainties. This was all very attractive and it was very successful when applied to technical matters. It seemed successful when applied to human affairs because judgement and certainty gave a basis for action and for right-eousness. In fact this habit of 'logic' is no less a belief system than any other. If you choose to look at the world in a certain way then you will reinforce your belief by seeing the world in that way.

So the trend has been to flee the world of perception in terms of thinking and to leave perception to art which could explore and elaborate perceptions at will. I believe it is time we did turn our attention to the world of perception in order to understand what actually happens in that world. The world of perception is closely related to the way the brain handles information and that is what I explore in the book *I am Right – You are Wrong*.

There is no 'game truth' in perception as there is in mathematics where something is true because it follows from the rules of the game and the universe. All truth in perception is either circular or provisional. Circular truth is like two people each telling the other that he or she is telling the truth. Provisional truth is based on experience: 'it seems to me'; 'as far as I can see'; 'in my experience'. There is none of that wonderful certainty which we have with ordinary logic – which is a 'belief truth' that masquerades as a 'game truth'.

In the inner world of perception there is not the solidity and permanence of 'rock logic'. A rock is hard, definite and permanent, and does not shift. This is the logic of 'is'. Instead, perception is based on water logic. Water flows. Water is not definite and hard edged but can adapt to its container. Water logic is based on 'to'.

The purpose of this book is to explore the nature and behaviour of water logic and to demonstrate some practical ways of using it.

Water logic is the logic of the inner world of perception. I suspect that it also applies, far more than we have hitherto thought, to the external world as well. As we start to examine self-organizing systems, as mathematics begins to look into non-linear systems and chaos, so we shall find that water logic is also relevant to many aspects of the external world to which we have always applied rock logic. I believe this to be the case with economics.

There is a direct impact of perception and water logic even on the apparent rock logic of science. The mind can see only what it is prepared to see. The analysis of data does not, by itself, produce ideas. The analysis of data can only allow us to select from existing ideas. There is a growing emphasis on the importance of hypotheses, speculation, provocation and model building, all of which allow us to see the world differently. The creation of these frameworks of possibility is a perceptual process.

I should add that there is no such thing as a contradiction in perception. Opposing views may be held in parallel. There is mismatch where something does not fit our expectations – like a black four-of-hearts playing card – but that is another matter.

Because of this ability of perception to hold contradictions, logic has been a very poor way of changing perceptions. Perceptions can be changed (by exploration, insight, context changes, atrophy, etc.) but not by logic. That is another very good reason for getting to understand perception.

Only a very small part of our lives is spent in mathematics or logical analysis. By far the greater part is spent dealing with perception. What we see on television and how we respond to it, is perception. Our notions of ecological dangers and the greenhouse effect are based on perception. Prejudice, racism, anti-semitism are all matters of perception. Conflicts that are not simply bully-boy power plays are based on misperceptions. Since perception is so important a part of our lives there seems merit in examining the nature of water logic rather than trying still harder to fit the world into our traditional rock logic.

WATER LOGIC

'Sad to think how much harm has been caused by the brutal arrogance of rock logic' – Dudley Herschbach, Nobel Prize, Professor of Chemistry at Harvard University. This quote was made casually in a personal letter to me. I asked Professor Herschbach if I could use it as a quote because it embraces so much in a simple sentence.

Rock is hard, unchanging and unyielding. A rock is of a definite shape. Water is gentler. Water is soft and yielding.

A rock can be used for attack and if attacked it is hard and solid. If you attack water it offers no resistance but then engulfs or drowns the attacker.

If you place a rock on a surface it sits there. A rock 'is'. If you pour water on to a flat surface it spreads out and 'explores'. If there is the slightest incline water 'flows'.

A rock does not change its shape depending on the surrounding circumstances. Water has no shape but adjusts to the container. A truth is very often a truth only in a certain context. Water logic emphasizes the importance of context.

If you have a lump of rock in a glass and tilt the glass the rock will eventually fall out. The rock is either in the glass or out of the glass. With water you can lose some water from the glass and still keep some in the glass – it does not have to be either/or.

If you add a rock to another rock you get two rocks. If you add water to water you do not get two waters. The new water combines with the old to give water. This additive aspect of water logic is very similar to the fuzzy logic that is now becoming so useful in artificial intelligence. Perceptions add up to a whole as in poetry.

Rock logic is often concerned with 'but' as we show how things differ. Water logic is more concerned with 'and' as we show how the inputs add up to a whole.

Western argument is very much based on the clash of rock logic. Japanese discussion is more based on the adding of further layers as in water logic.

All the above give an impression of the difference between rock logic and water logic. The simplest way to summarize it is to say that rock logic is based on 'is' and water logic is based on 'to' – What does this flow to? What does this lead to? What does this add up to?

Traditional rock logic is based on identity: 'This is a caterpillar.' It is also based on 'have' and 'inclusion': 'This caterpillar is green and has a hairy body.' Inclusion, exclusion, identity and non-identity, and contradiction are the very stuff of reasoning. We create boxes in the forms of categories, classifications and words. We judge whether something belongs in a certain box and if it does we can give it all the characteristics of that box. This is the basis of our judgement and our certainty and it serves us well even though it can lead to 'brutal arrogance'.

In place of this 'is' of rock logic we put the 'to' of water logic.

'TO'

What do we mean by 'to'? A ball on a slope rolls 'to' or towards the bottom of the slope. A river flows 'to' the sea. A path leads 'to' some place.

An egg in a frying-pan changes 'to' a fried egg.

A falling egg leads 'to' the mess of a broken egg on the carpet.

A film director may cut from a shot of a falling egg 'to' a shot of a collapsing tower.

A film director may cut from a shot of a falling egg 'to' a shot of an anguished girl.

A ball that rolls 'to' a new position is still the same ball. The raw egg that becomes the fried egg is still the same egg in a different form. But the shot of the collapsing tower or the anguished girl in the film is only related to the prior shot of the falling egg because the director has chosen to relate them.

So we really use 'to' in a number of different ways.

Throughout this book I intend to use 'to' in a very simple and clear sense: what does this lead to? What happens next?

It simply means what happens next in time. If a film image of an egg is followed by the image of an elephant then the egg leads to the elephant. If you are being driven in a car along a scenic route and an idyllic shot of a cottage is followed by a view of a power station, then that is what happens next. So the sense of 'to' is not limited to 'becoming' or 'changing to', although this will also be included in the very broad definition of 'to' as what happens next. An unstable system can become a stable system. A stable system can become an unstable system. One thing leads to another.

Because this notion of 'to' is so very important it would be useful to define it precisely with a new word. Perhaps we could create a new preposition, 'leto', to indicate 'leads to'. At this point in time it would sound only artificial and unnecessary.

A woman brings her faulty electric kettle to a store and asks for a replacement. The sales assistant knows the kettle could never have been bought at that store because the store does not stock that brand. But the sales assistant changes the kettle for a new one. On any basis of 'is' logic and justice this must seem absurd. But in 'to' logic it does make sense. The woman is so delighted that she becomes a regular customer. Research in the USA has shown that money spent in this way is returned fivefold. The traditional logician would argue that next day there will be a long queue of people outside with all their faulty appliances. What then? Well, the store is under no obligation to replace them. The situation is different and will be assessed at that moment. There is no need to be locked into a course of action. I used this story in my book *I am Right – You are Wrong* and I repeat it here in order to link the mention of water logic in that book to its fuller exploration in this book.

We now know that in self-organizing systems provocation is mathematically essential in order to disturb one stable state so that we may arrive at a better stable state. This point was elaborated in 1983 by Dr Scott Kirkpatrick of IBM. It is similar to provocations and the use of the word 'po' which I had been advocating since 1970. In lateral thinking we may use a provocation in order to destabilize the system or to get us out of the usual perception channels. For example we might say: 'Po a car has square wheels.' If we were then to use judgement we would have to reject this idea because it 'is' wrong. But instead of judgement we use 'movement' which is a flow operation. We look to see where this provocation 'leads to'. The bumpiness of a square wheel is predictable so suspension adjusting in keeping would give a smooth ride. This leads on to the idea of suspension that adjusts to the bumpiness of the ground so giving what is now called 'active' or 'intelligent' suspension. The deliberate use of provocation followed by 'movement' is one of the techniques of lateral thinking.

When I used argument and negativity to attack the prevalence of argument and negativity, I was accused – correctly – of making use of the very methods I was attacking. Let us see where this line of thinking leads to. If negativity cannot be used to attack negativity then negativity can never be attacked! My point of view is that argument and negativity do have a limited value for certain purposes, one of which is to attack argument and negativity. I see no need for the absolute either/or positions of rock logic.

Our current concept of democracy locks us into the historic way of conducting democracy. Anything else is judged as not being 'democracy'. Yet we could imagine a system in which those whose votes best represented the mix of the electorate, got elected. For example in a 70 per cent white and 30 per cent black area the candidates nearest to the 70–30 support would win. There would need to be voter registration along party or ethnic lines. Rock logic would be concerned with how this idea fits our existing habits of democracy. Water logic would be concerned with what it 'leads to'.

Pragmatism is very much based on the 'leads to' of water logic. There is a justified fear of pragmatism because it seems to seek to operate without principles. This is nonsense because the principles can be just as much part of the pragmatism as are the circumstances. One strong reason for a dislike of pragmatism is the fear that 'the end may come to justify the means'. In other words if the end is worthwhile then the means of achieving that end are justified. Since different people and different bodies will have different notions of worthwhile ends the result would be chaos and barbarity. Interestingly the very reason we reject this notion of the end justifying the means, is a pure example of pragmatism and water logic. We are concerned with what it 'will lead to'. So pragmatism can police pragmatism just as well as rock logic polices rock logic.

What is a pen? It 'is' an instrument for writing. We could also analyse the pen in terms of its physical nature and component parts: nib, ink reservoir, body, cap, etc. This tells us what a pen 'is'. But the value of a pen is highly dependent on the context. A pen is not much use to a person who cannot write. A pen at that moment is of great value to someone who needs to write an urgent medical prescription or a vital telephone number. A pen used to sign a treaty has historic value. A pen can be an expensive gift. All these different values arise as we flow on from the pen itself 'to' its use.

London may be sixty miles away but you may be driving on a road which is called 'London Road'. This is because the road leads to London. So the road is defined by where it gets you. A road or path is a classic example of 'to' because each point leads on 'to' the next point. We are more likely to follow the path than stray off it.

Consider the sequences of letters shown in fig. 1. In each case the letter C is exactly the same. It has the same shape and it is produced in the same way. But according to water logic each of the four Cs is different because each 'leads to' a different letter: CD, CA, CX, CE. This may seem absurd until we realize that even in pronunciation

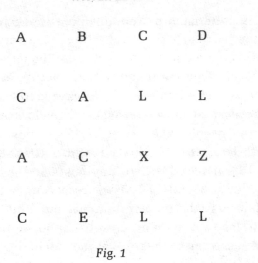

Fig. 1

there is a difference: the C in CALL is pronounced differently from the C in CELL.

Rock logic would say that the sequences are different because they are made up of different letters. It is actually water logic which says they are also different because they 'lead to' different ideas. The first sequence leads us on to the alphabet with a predictable sequence of letters. The second sequence leads us on to the word CALL and its meaning. The third appears to be a random selection but we could figure out that it is the first and third letter of the alphabet moving forward from the beginning and the last and third from the last moving back from the end. The final sequence is another word CELL and here we could be led in two different directions: cell as in a monk's cell or prison cell; and cell as in the cells that make up human tissue. The complex patterns of perception are made up from where a stimulus 'leads to'.

Far be it from me to claim that people do not already use water logic and have not always done so. There are many occasions on which water logic is used and there are many people who use water logic most of the time. Nevertheless, the established and legitimate logic has always been rock logic. In any sustained argument only rock logic is acceptable. Many women have told me that they find water logic more natural but that they always seem to lose out in an argument – because that is a game played according to the rules of rock logic.

My intention is to legitimize water logic and to indicate its place and value as the logic of perception. I shall attempt to legitimize water logic not simply by drawing attention to its value but by showing the underlying basis for it in the natural behaviour of the brain.

There were lateral thoughts before I introduced the term 'lateral thinking'. There were people who had a special aptitude and inclination for lateral thinking. My contribution was to legitimize lateral thinking as a useful and necessary part of thinking. When my first book was published, many people who were highly creative in their own fields were the first to write to me to express an interest in lateral thinking. I showed that the need for lateral thinking arose directly from the pattern-making and pattern-using behaviour of the brain because there was a need to cut 'laterally' across the usual patterns. From this basis I designed specific tools which could be used systematically and deliberately in order to generate new ideas. In the same way I shall propose some methods for carrying through water logic.

DANCE OF THE JELLYFISH

I ask the reader to read this section in the simple and direct manner in which it is written. For the moment, do not try to relate the obvious analogy to anything else. That would weaken your grasp of the analogy and only lead to confusion at this point. Treat the jellyfish as jellyfish.

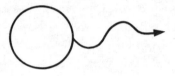

Fig. 2

As shown in fig. 2, each jellyfish consists of a round body and a single tentacle with a barbed sting at the other end. You may feel that this is more like a spermatazoa than a jellyfish but it is a very special sort of jellyfish.

As shown in fig. 3, the barbed sting of the jellyfish can be thrust into the jelly body of another jellyfish – but never, quite sensibly, into its own body. The sting is inserted fully into the body of the other jellyfish and cannot be withdrawn or used for any further purpose.

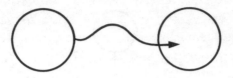

Fig. 3

We can suppose that this sort of stinging behaviour is not vicious but is in fact benign. It is a form of making contact, of communication, and of companionship.

Each jellyfish has but one sting and can therefore only sting one other jellyfish. But the body of a jellyfish can receive stings from any number of other jellyfish. We could suppose that the more popular the jellyfish the more friends and communication it will have, so the more stings it will receive.

We have now set up a simple system with simple rules. This is really a rather special 'universe' populated solely by these special jellyfish with their defined rules of behaviour. We can now set about exploring some of the things that might happen in this special universe.

Obviously the jellyfish can arrange or organize themselves in a number of different ways. We can look at some of these ways.

Fig. 4

Fig. 4 shows a simple 'chain' leading from *A* to *B*. One jellyfish stings another and the second stings a third, and so on. The chain could extend through many jellyfish. There is a chain, link or path from *A* to *B*. This may be the simplest form of organization in this universe.

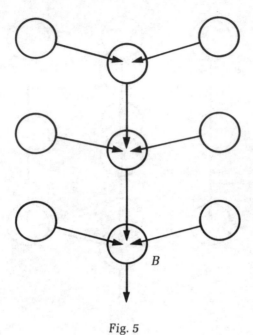

Fig. 5

Fig. 5 now shows a modification of the basic chain arrangement. There are now side chains which link into the main chain. This is a sort of 'river valley' arrangement. It is what you might see as you fly over Switzerland. The main chain represents the main river valley and the side chains represent the tributaries flowing in from the hills around. This arrangement would be very good at 'draining' a whole area so that everything ends up at B.

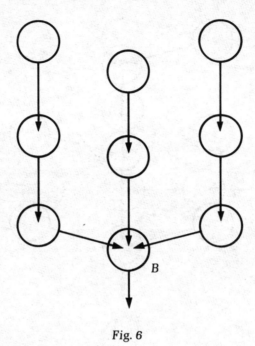

Fig. 6

Fig. 6 shows another drainage arrangement. This time the chains or flow-channels remain separate throughout their length and only join up right at the end. The result is still to drain the area into B.

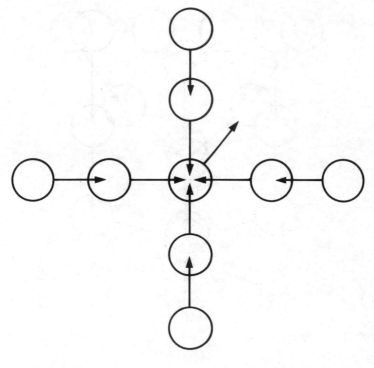

Fig. 7

The 'star' arrangement shown in fig. 7 is really no more than a rearrangement of the chains shown in fig. 6 so that they radiate out from a central node. Everything is now drained towards the centre along the flow-channel tentacles.

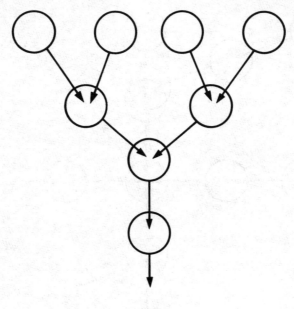

Fig. 8

The arrangement shown in fig. 8 is a little different from both previous arrangements. It is a 'tree' arrangement. The topmost level of jellyfishes is like the leaves of a tree. These arise from a small branch. The small branches arise from a bigger branch. The bigger branches arise from the trunk of the tree. The main point is that the jellyfishes are brought together in a hierarchical organization. We could consider it also as a large funnel which is draining into the trunk of the tree. Every tree you look at could be looked at in the same way.

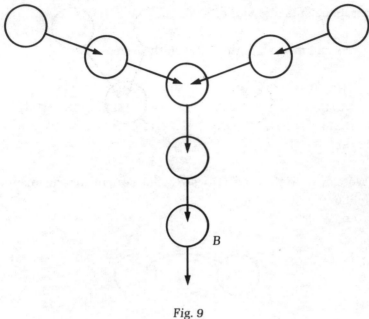

Fig. 9

Fig. 9 shows a very simple 'funnel' arrangement which
is actually simpler than the preceding arrangement. An
input entering the system at any point will be passed
along to end up at B. This arrangement could also be
considered a side-view of the arrangement shown in fig. 8.
I shall be returning to this simplified funnel arrangement
later.

At this point we add another simple rule to the behaviour of the special jellyfish. A jellyfish *must* insert its
sting into the body of another jellyfish. No sting can be

left free and unused – as has been the case in all the arrangements shown here.

We can now state the jellyfish theorem:

THE BODY OF THE JELLYFISH CAN RECEIVE ANY NUMBER OF STINGS BUT THE JELLYFISH MUST INSERT ITS SOLE STING INTO THE BODY OF ANOTHER JELLYFISH.

We can now proceed and see what sort of arrangements follow.

Fig. 10

The simplest arrangement is the 'embrace' in which two jellyfishes just sting each other. There is a certain completeness to this mutual adulation. There is no need – and no place – for any more jellyfish. The two are totally wrapped up in each other.

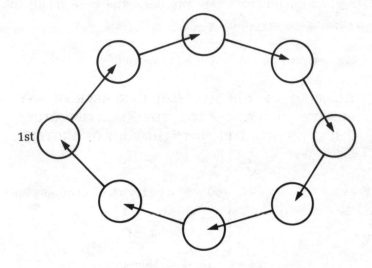

Fig. 11

The next arrangement is the 'daisy-chain'. This is simply a chain in which the free sting at the end of the chain now loops back to sting the first jellyfish in the chain. The communication passes around and around in an endless loop – as in the game of pass the parcel.

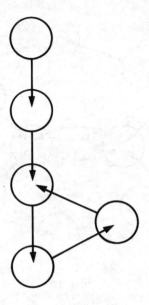

Fig. 12

In fig. 12 the free sting at the end of a chain does not go all the way back to sting the first jellyfish in the chain but only loops part of the way back. The result is a mini-circle or mini-daisy-chain with a feeder chain attached. Note that this feeder chain feeds into the loop but then plays no part in the loop thereafter.

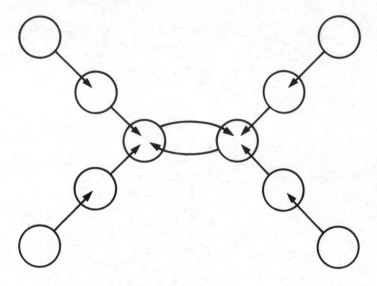

Fig. 13

Fig. 13 is only a more complicated version of the previous arrangement. At the centre there is an embrace. Into
this embrace feed four feeder chains. Any of the previous
arrangements showing a free sting can become arrangements in which the free sting is inserted into any other
jellyfish to form a small loop or an embrace. The rest of
the arrangement then merely acts as a feeder or drainage
arrangement.

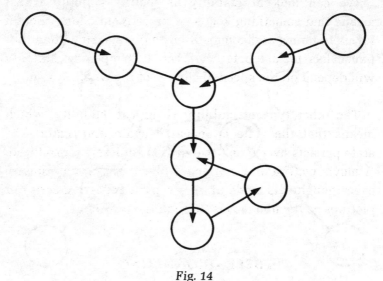

Fig. 14

Fig. 14 shows the simple funnel arrangement that we saw previously in fig. 9. This time the free sting at the end has looped back to form a mini-circle. This means that an input at any point in the funnel will always end up in the stable repeating loop at the outlet of the funnel.

STABILITY

The embrace, the daisy-chain and mini-daisy-chain all represent repeating loops. The message would be carried around the loop endlessly. In terms of the jellyfish universe this represents a 'stable state'. All other states are transient and unstable but the loop is stable. So, eventually all other states will end up in some loop or other.

We can look at stability as 'pause' stability which means that something keeps its present state long enough for us to notice and comment on that state. How long that pause has to last before we call it 'temporary' stability will depend on the speed of change of the whole system.

The other type of stability is 'repeat' stability, which means that the state is repeated again and again. The state persists over time because it is endlessly reproduced. A movie picture of a stationary object appears stationary even though it is made up of a rapidly repeating series of pictures as the film moves through the projector.

SELF-ORGANIZING

If a number of jellyfish were put into a container and left to their own devices we would inevitably get an arrangement similar to the ones shown here. There would be feeder chains and a stable loop. It is possible that the whole could form into one stable loop. It is possible that there may be two or more separate arrangements. Indeed, each pair could form an embrace with no further contact with any other jellyfish. What we could say with certainty is that the system would organize itself into a stable state. This is one form of a self-organizing system. There is no mystery about it.

HOW THE BRAIN FLOWS INTO
PERCEPTION

We can now transfer the dance of the jellyfish into that behaviour of the brain which gives rise to perception.

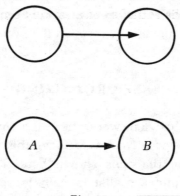

Fig. 15

The upper part of fig. 15 shows a jellyfish with its sting inserted into the body of another jellyfish. At this point we leave the jellyfish and convert the sting into a simple arrow to indicate a direction of flow. We now have two circles with an arrow going from one to the other. Each circle now represents a 'state' or condition. In the case of the brain this would represent a state of nerve activity. You might say that anything we could capture in a photograph at any moment would be a 'state'. Someone might move from a state of anger to a state of punching someone. This might be succeeded by a further state in which the victim punched back.

So the lower part of fig. 15 shows how state A leads to state B. We are now back to water logic and 'flow', 'leads to' and 'to'. State A is succeeded by state B.

What do these states mean in terms of what is actually happening in the brain? Fig. 16 shows what appears to be a mountain at the end of a range of lower hills.

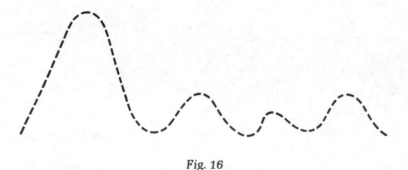

Fig. 16

The mountain represents an area of peak nerve activity in the brain. This need not be one physical area but a group of interconnected nerves wherever they are. The low hills represent areas which would have been active but are suppressed by the activity of the peak of the moment.

We now come to a 'tiring factor'. A weightlifter could not continue to hold a heavy weight for more than a few minutes. The weightlifter would tire and put the weight down. After a rest he might pick up the weight again. Nerves tire in the same way. They run out of energy, the necessary enzymes are deactivated, etc. This tiring factor is an important part of the behaviour of the brain. It is so fundamental that I suspect that different rates of tiring probably have an effect on such things as intelligence and even some mental illnesses.

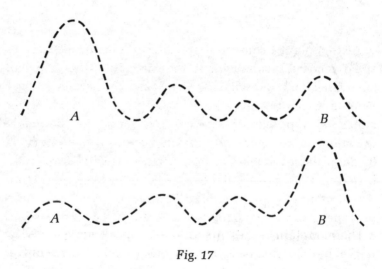

Fig. 17

As the peak of activity at A tires, so another potential peak at B, which has been suppressed, now becomes active as a peak and in turn suppresses A. This transition is shown in fig. 17. So we can see how state A has been succeeded by state B. In other words state A has flowed to state B. State A has gone and state B is present. We can represent this with the simple notation shown in fig. 18, which is the notation we had before.

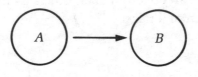

Fig. 18

At this point I come to a procedural dilemma. There are some readers, probably not the majority, who will ask such questions as: what do you mean by nerve activity? Why is there only one state of activity? Why should other states be suppressed? And so on. These are legitimate questions. I have gone into the answers to these questions in detail in my book *The Mechanism of Mind* (first published in 1969 and available as a Penguin book, and more recently in my book *I am Right – You are Wrong*. It would be repetitious to go into these matters here and would detract from the main development of the theme. Those who want the details should read one of the books mentioned, preferably the more recent one.

The main point is that the nerve circuits of the brain offer a system in which one state of activity (defined as a connected group of activated units) is succeeded by another, and so on.

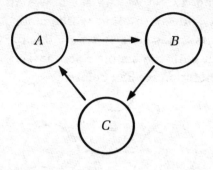

Fig. 19

Fig. 19 shows a situation in which there is 'flow' from *A* to *B* and then to *C* and then back to *A*. This can be represented by the standard notation, as shown in fig. 18, and we have the same sort of repeating loop we had with the jellyfish.

We can now continue with the simple notation of states that lead to other states. Just as a jellyfish can sting only one other jellyfish, so, under a particular set of circumstances, any state will always flow to one other state.

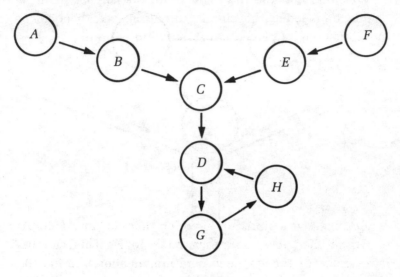

Fig. 20

We can start by looking at the simple 'funnel' arrangement, as shown in fig. 20. The states A, B, C, E, F, are all unstable and all drain into the stable repeating loop D–G–H.

We could now return to look at all the jellyfish arrange-ments and, using the simpler notation, see them all as possible types of perceptual activity in the brain.

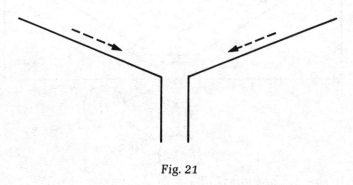

Fig. 21

This is exactly what we would get in a funnel, as shown in fig. 21, where everything drains towards the centre.

Fig. 22 shows a very flat, almost two-dimensional funnel placed in a box with a lid in which there are holes marked S, T, U, V, W, and X. If you drop a small steel ball through hole S the ball will roll down the funnel and end up at Z. If you drop the ball through hole X you will also end up at Z. It is obvious that wherever you drop the ball you will always record Z.

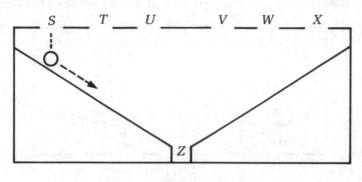

Fig. 22

If you did not know about the funnel you would regard this as very strange behaviour. Whatever the input the result was always Z. This is in total contrast to expected behaviour – and our normal understanding of information systems – for we expect to record exactly what we have put into the system. This is shown in fig. 23, in which the funnel has been replaced by a tray of sand. In such a system an input of A is recorded as A, and an input of F is recorded as F just as a camera records what is in front of it.

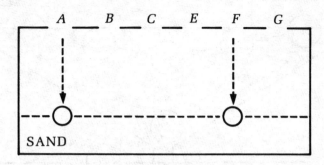

Fig. 23

So the funnel system shifts information around. In fact it is an 'active' information system in contrast to the 'passive' system which just records what is presented. The funnel system of nerve activity, repeated in fig. 24 for convenience, behaves exactly like the mechanical funnel. Any input will always end up in the stable state D–G–H.

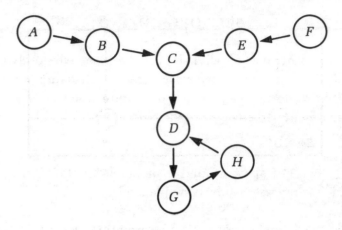

Fig. 24

There is, of course, no need whatever for the arms of
the funnel to be sloping since gravity is not involved. I
have simply drawn them that way to make it easier to
think of the funnel effect. All the jellyfish arrangements
that give a 'drainage' function ('tree', 'river', 'star', etc.), all
behave in the same way.

This is how perceptions are formed and this is why
perceptions are so very stable. An input may occur in a
variety of forms but will eventually settle down and stabilize in one form. That is the perception we recognize and
use. All the others are unstable, intermediate effects.

SELF-ORGANIZING

Just as a number of jellyfish in a container would always end up organizing themselves into a structure with a stable repeating loop in it, so a finite number of nerve states will also always organize itself into a stable condition.

In fig. 25 I show a number of potential states, each of which is represented by a simple circle.

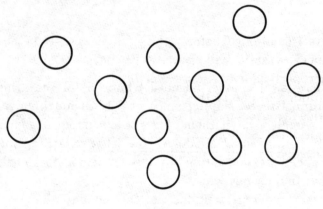

Fig. 25

The circles are now joined up with random lines, as shown in fig. 26. It does not really matter how the lines are placed because they simply represent potential paths between different states. You could have a line from each circle to every other circle but it would look rather messy.

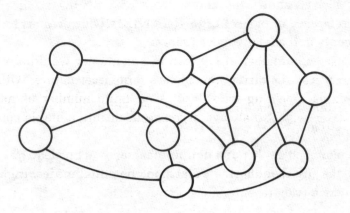

Fig. 26

As I mentioned before, under any given set of circumstances, a state will 'lead to' or 'be succeeded by' one other particular state. So we put a double slash at the beginning of one of the potential paths to show that this is the favoured path. The second choice is shown by a single slash. So in fig. 27 state *A* is much more likely to be succeeded by state *B* than by state *C*.

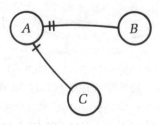

Fig. 27

Fig. 28 shows the states redrawn with the slashes of preference in place. I urge you to draw your own arrangements in the following sequence:

1. Put down a random arrangement of circles.

2. Connect them up randomly (at least two lines to each circle).

3. For each circle put a double slash on one line leaving the circle, and a single slash on one other line leaving the circle.

I want to emphasize that I have not designed this in any special way whatever.

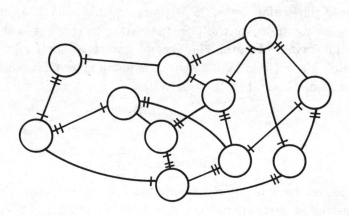

Fig. 28

At this point, take a pencil and, entering the system at any circle, follow a path. You must always exit from a circle along the line with a double slash. If you happen to enter a circle along the double slash line you must exit along the single slash line (this is the second preference). See what you end up with.

Fig. 29 shows the path that I took and what happened. It is very clear that there is a stable repeating loop and that all other states are unstable and feed into this loop.

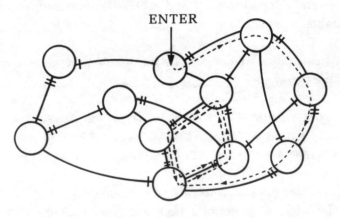

ENTER

Fig. 29

So, we have a self-organizing system that explains the mystery of perception: how it is that the brain can form stable perceptions from the chaos of the world around? The way the brain is organized makes it *inevitable* that stable perceptions will form whatever the input. Once these perception flows have formed, then we shall in future see the world in that way, just as the funnel system always ended up with the same result.

The behaviour of self-organizing systems is extremely simple once we get to treat them as self-organizing systems. If we do not make this jump but treat them in the old-fashioned way then they seem immensely complex. It is in the old-fashioned way that we have always tended to look at the brain.

Two further examples of the self-organizing system are shown in figs. 30 and 31. If you enter the system at any point and follow the preferred routes you will end up with a stable repeating loop.

At this point we could state de Bono's theorem – a very simple theorem:

FROM ANY INPUT A SYSTEM WITH A FINITE NUMBER OF STABLE STATES AND A TIRING FACTOR WILL ALWAYS REACH A STABLE REPEATING PATTERN.

It is so obvious that it hardly seems worth stating. Yet the implications of something that seems very simple can be extensive. I believe that to be the case here. The theorem is so obvious in hindsight that I suspect it exists already in another form – but if not, it is certainly worth having.

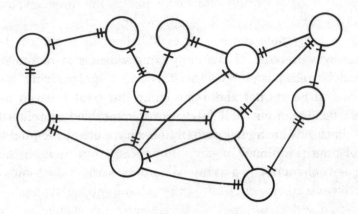

Fig. 30

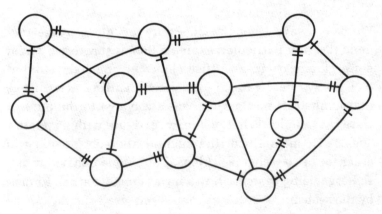

Fig. 31

THE BEHAVIOUR OF PERCEPTION

Using the above considerations as a base we can move forward to understand some of the fundamental behaviour of perception such as recognition, centring and preparedness.

RECOGNITION

Once the stable pattern is established, in terms of the pathway preferences, then any input which is at all similar will be recognized. The thing to be recognized does not have to be exactly the same or in the same position as before. The input will feed into the established pattern. This makes biological recognition very much more powerful than traditional or computer recognition (though this is now changing by making computers work in the biological way).

CENTRING

We can always recognize the 'pure' or 'ideal' image that underlies any particular example. For instance we might see a garden chair, an office chair, an armchair, etc. but will always be aware of the chair. Centring also means that in abstract matters we will always go to the pure or classic example. What we now end up with is Plato's 'ideals'. He maintained that such ideals must pre-exist in order for us to recognize things. The simple behaviour of a self-organizing system shows how such ideals are formed by the system.

PREPAREDNESS

The mind can only see what it is prepared to see. This is now widely accepted. That is why there is such a need for hypotheses, speculation, and provocation when examining data. Without such new 'frameworks' we would only be able to see the data in the old way.

All these matters which I have only hinted at here are examined in detail in the book *I am Right – You are Wrong.*

DISCRIMINATION

Fig. 32 shows yet another illustration of the self-organizing system. But this time there is a difference.

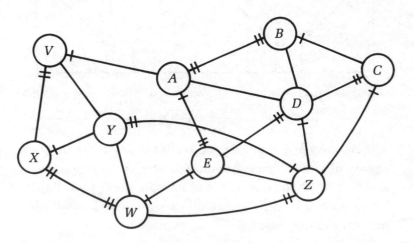

Fig. 32

The difference is that the system does not stabilize into one repeating loop but forms two loops: A–B–C–D–E and W–X–Y–Z. If you enter at one point you would end up with one loop and if you entered at another point you would end up with the other loop. If you were to enter at several points at once then you would end up with both loops. This simple system can now 'see the world' in one of two ways. This is the same as having the funnel-box with two funnels instead of one – as shown here in fig. 33. This box is capable of two perceptions.

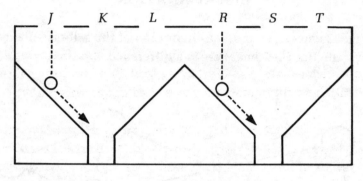

Fig. 33

If the two perceptions occur simultaneously then, for a variety of reasons (remote and recent past, emotions, etc.) one will be slightly more dominant and will be followed by an apparent 'shift of attention'. A connexion between the two will also be made.

MEANING

It may seem strange that so far I have not made much use of the word 'meaning' even though this must seem so essential to flow, water logic and perception. The reason is that I have wanted to establish the basis for meaning before making use of what is otherwise just a descriptive term.

In the tree type of organization that we first came across with the jellyfish, each of the leaves eventually feeds down into the trunk. That is exactly what happens in meaning. We feed in from the periphery to a central theme or meaning. This is shown again in fig. 34. Obviously we can go on adding to the leaves as further experience feeds into the same meaning.

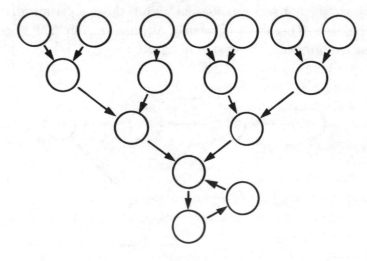

Fig. 34

THE IMPORTANCE OF WORDS

What I am going to suggest now is pure speculation or provocation even though it arises directly from the sort of considerations that have been examined here. Many people have suggested that language was essential for the development of thinking. I do not believe this to be strictly so because it is possible to think with pictures, and also children often think beyond the limits of their vocabulary. But language may have helped in the development of thinking in quite a different way by providing one end of the stabilizing loop in perception. We could go from the messy perception to the language sound and back to the perception and so on in the sort of repeating loop we have been looking at. In other words language may have helped by stabilizing perceptions and giving them a certain discreteness. This is an extremely useful function. The suggested process is illustrated in fig. 35.

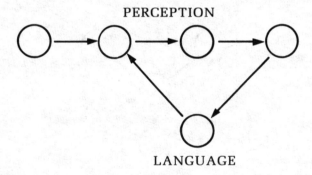

Fig. 35

The downside, as I have discussed extensively in the other book, is that language does force us to look at the world in the traditional ways which may have become obsolete.

MYTHS AND 'WHY?'

Younger children continually ask, 'Why?' They are not looking for a causal explanation in the adult sense of science. They want 'connectors'. They are looking for ways of filling in gaps and connecting up experience so that they can get a more stable whole. This process is suggested in fig. 36.

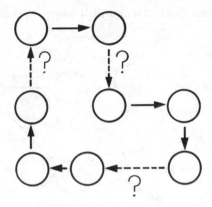

Fig. 36

If there are no parents around to provide the connectors demanded by the question 'why?', then the children have to create their own explanations and myths. The myths formed by adults who have no one to ask are of exactly the same nature. The history of science is full of connecting myths: 'malaria' means the bad air from the swamp that gave people malaria. For a long time there was the theory of 'phlogiston' to explain why things burned. Other myths of witches, ghosts, dragons and fair princesses have a somewhat similar basis. Some myths do have other values as crystallizations or metaphors to preserve certain values and behaviour ideals.

The function of myths as connectors has a real value even if the myths are nonsense. In perception truth is only 'circularity' and the relationship to the outside world is irrelevant for the moment. The purpose of the outside world is to improve myths.

The role of myth as connector is suggested in fig. 37.

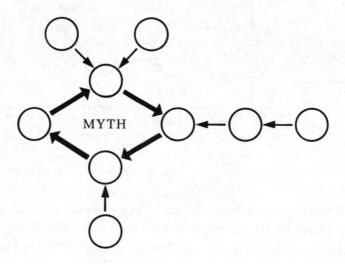

Fig. 37

A long time ago I suggested that we might need a powerful word in language to act as a mini-myth to connect things up. We do use the word 'something' for this purpose but that is a weak way of doing it.

CLOSURE

The word 'closure' brings to mind traditional gestalt psychologists who, in my view, were on the right track even though they talked about matters in a vague and descriptive manner. They had their own myths of explanation.

Any self-organizing system of the type described here will settle down into some repeating stable loop. This probably takes place at a number of different levels as I shall discuss very shortly.

One of the most difficult things in teaching or in any attempt to change perceptions is the enlargement of a loop. If a person is happy with the stability of a tight loop, as shown in fig. 38, then that person will be extremely reluctant to shift to the wider loop. It does not matter that the tight loop is full of myths and prejudices. It is the completeness of the loop or 'early closure' that matters. Once again perceptual truth is system truth (stable circularity) and not measurement truth.

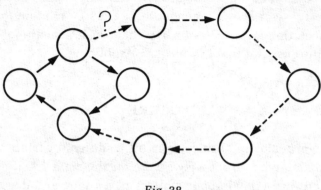

Fig. 38

If loops are so very stable, then how do loops ever shift?

SHIFT

If there is a biochemical shift in the brain then the preferred path may no longer be from *A* to *B* but may now be from *A* to *C*. The circumstances or context have changed. Emotions can probably produce such changes in biochemical background. The process is suggested in fig. 39.

There can be other causes for a change in circumstances. Further inputs may alter the sensitivity of other nerve groups to activation so the number of potential states is altered and there are different pathways in action. It is hardly surprising that if we look at a different scene we see different things.

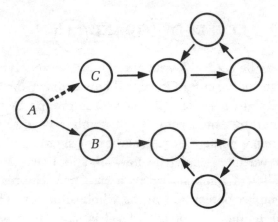

Fig. 39

It is possible that there is also a tiring factor for repeating loops as well as for nerve groups. This would mean that we would move on from one loop to another loop and each state would merely represent a loop. This could be associated with a sort of 'boredom' factor. I suspect that boredom is not just the absence of stimulation but actually plays a key role in brain mechanics and may even have a biochemical equivalent.

Once we start to look at shift then the functional difference between pause stability and repeat stability tends to disappear because if a repeating loop only lasts for a limited time the effect is the same as a pause. The way the stability is set up is, however, totally different.

LEVELS OF ORGANIZATION

There may be several levels of organization involved. First there is the nerve circuit level and how connected neurones (nerves) might stabilize themselves as groups. A number of these groups then establish a stable repeating loop to give a simple perception. A rotation of simple perceptions is what we might call the flow of attention – and this might follow a track set up by experience. The result is a more complex perception of the whole situation. To determine the boundaries of each level is more an exercise in descriptive philosophy than in system behaviour.

Possible levels of organization are suggested in fig. 40, but I would not attach too much importance to this.

BROAD PRINCIPLES OF SYSTEM BEHAVIOUR

We do not yet know the detailed workings of the brain. But I believe that we do know enough about the broad principles of brain behaviour. This is behaviour as a self-organizing information system. I believe that from this understanding we can get useful understanding and insights and also design effective thinking tools (for example the tools of lateral thinking). At this point are we talking about philosophy, experimental psychology, mathematics or what?

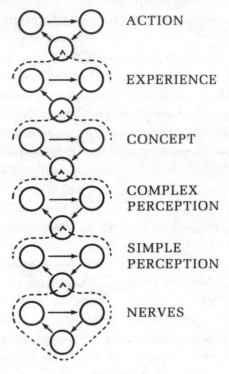

ACTION

EXPERIENCE

CONCEPT

COMPLEX
PERCEPTION

SIMPLE
PERCEPTION

NERVES

Fig. 40

Philosophy tends to be descriptive and analyses the words we use for description. Experimental psychology can measure tiny fractions of the whole but needs to be driven by concepts of system organization.

Behaviour within a defined universe is really mathematics. So what I am writing about in this book is a sort of mathematics: that is the behaviour within systems with a finite number of states and flow between these states. In physics we happily accept a divide between the conceptual models of theoretical physics and the measurements of experimental physics. Perhaps we need a new word, 'mentics', to cover the exploration of defined information systems. There is nothing magical about what I am laying out. It is fully compatible with the most elementary behaviour of what we know about nerve circuits. What we need to explore is the power of simple organizational behaviour because simple systems can be very powerful. It is that exploration which I am carrying out here and elsewhere.

It is quite obvious that the explorations carried out in this section are directly based on water logic. The base of the system is the simple flow from state A to state B. In the rest of the book I shall be focusing on the practical application of water logic. It was, however, necessary to consider here how water logic is the functioning and organizing logic of perception. I hope you have not had difficulty in understanding this section. I have tried to be as explicit as possible at the risk of being repetitious. It is essentially very simple and difficulty usually arises with people who want to overcomplicate matters. If, however, you have not fully understood the section, then you can still move on to the practical matters and use these practical processes directly in their own right.

FLOWSCAPES

If you are at the top of a mountain the landscape is spread out before you. You can fly over the landscape and get a good overall impression from a plane or, better, from a helicopter. A painter could lay out a landscape in a picture. Models of a landscape could be used to show a new development scheme. An experienced eye could immediately see the landscape from the contour lines on a map. A landscape is for looking at the land, for looking at the terrain.

In an exactly similar way a 'flowscape' is for looking at flow. Flow is the essence of water logic, so in a flowscape we look directly at water logic. We see it as in a picture or a map. In this way we get to 'see' our thinking. It is as if we were standing outside our own thinking and looking at it objectively. We can then start noticing things about it just as we notice things about a landscape. Later on we might try to intervene in order to see what could be done to change our thinking – or to change the situation.

Essentially a flowscape is a picture of our inner world. It is a picture of our perception. It is possible to construct a flowscape for the outer world but this has then to be specified. A flowscape is a picture of our perception as it is at the moment. We make a flowscape in order to understand our perception.

A flowscape is extremely easy to put together. It is important to follow the steps, one at a time, without trying to jump ahead. It is also important to be honest and not to contrive the result you think you want.

STREAM OF CONSCIOUSNESS LIST

The first step is to decide the subject for the flowscape. As an example let us suppose your neighbour is playing music too loudly late in the evening.

The second step is to put down a 'stream of consciousness' list. You put points down in a list, each point on a separate line. A stream of consciousness implies aspects, ideas, items, features and factors that occur to you. There is not a systematic analysis. I call it 'stream of consciousness' to indicate the ideas that occur to you as you consider the situation. These ideas are not solution suggestions but just aspects of the situation. I shall deal with this 'stream of consciousness' more fully in the next section.

So for the neighbourly music the stream of consciousness list might look like this:

LOUD MUSIC

PERSISTENT

CANNOT SLEEP

NO RESPONSE TO COMPLAINTS

NEIGHBOUR IS DISMISSIVE

THREATS DO NOT WORK

AGGRESSIVE NEIGHBOUR

NO ONE ELSE IS AFFECTED

GOING ON FOR A LONG TIME

IMPOSSIBLE TO BLOCK OUT MUSIC

This is a genuine 'top of the head' list of factors. I put down the factors as they occurred to me for the imagined situation. With further thought the list might have been different. The main point is that this is a genuine stream of consciousness list. There would be no point in carefully choosing the points in order to demonstrate a result.

The third step is to go through the list giving each item a letter from the alphabet as an indicator: *A, B, C, D,* etc.

The fourth step is the most important one and involves the 'flow' part. Taking the items on the list one at a time you see to which other item on the list the chosen item 'flows'. Quite simply, to which other item does this lead? It is not a matter of cause and effect but 'what comes to mind next'. This may be very easy because another item offers an obvious destination. Or it may be difficult because two or more other items seem possible destinations. Or there may be no item which seems a natural destination. In any case do your best.

For example we have:

A   LOUD MUSIC

This seems to lead to item *C* so we now put:

A   LOUD MUSIC   *C*

We can take another item:

E   NEIGHBOUR IS DISMISSIVE

This seems to lead on to *F*, so we have:

E   NEIGHBOUR IS DISMISSIVE   *F*

The whole list might now look as follows:

A   LOUD NOISE   *C*

B   PERSISTENT   *C*

C   CANNOT SLEEP   *H*

D   NO RESPONSE TO COMPLAINTS   *E*

E   NEIGHBOUR IS DISMISSIVE   F

F   THREATS DO NOT WORK   G

G   AGGRESSIVE NEIGHBOUR   E

H   NO ONE ELSE IS AFFECTED   F

I   GOING ON FOR A LONG TIME   C

J   IMPOSSIBLE TO BLOCK OUT MUSIC   C

The fifth step is to make the flowscape using the letters to represent the items. For example, if A, LOUD NOISE, flows to C, CANNOT SLEEP, then we simply indicate that A flows to C as shown in fig. 41.

Fig. 41

We carry this out for all the points. In doing this it is helpful to see which items are listed most often on the right hand side (as destinations). In this example, C is listed five times. Put down the most used destination first and then see which items flow to that destination.

Be sure that each letter is put down only once on the flowscape. Check this from time to time as it is quite easy to put down the same letter more than once.

The first time around the flowscape will look rather messy. So you just redraw it in a neater way so that the arrows do not cross each other.

The final result is a neatly laid out flowscape as shown in fig. 42. As can be seen in this flowscape, each item (represented by its letter) flows on to another item.

Some items receive many inputs – like C. But each letter can only have a single arrow going from it to another letter. This is very important. It is the same as the jellyfish rule that a jellyfish could only sting one other jellyfish. It is based on the general rule that under a particular set of circumstances a state will always flow to one other state.

For the moment we shall assume a fixed context or set of circumstances. Later we shall see what happens when the context is changed.

The steps for constructing the flowscape are summarized here:

1. Decide on the subject.

2. Draw up a stream of consciousness list.

3. Give each item a letter of the alphabet.

4. For each item indicate the flow to another item: put the relevant letter.

5. Draw the flowscape.

6. Redraw the flowscape, tidying it up.

EXAMINING THE FLOWSCAPE

Now that we have the flowscape we can look at it and comment upon it just as we might comment upon a landscape. We can notice a number of features at once.

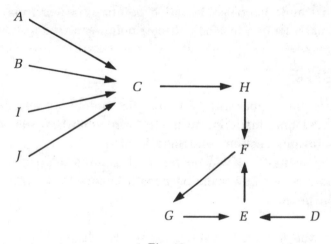

Fig. 42

COLLECTORS

These are points which seem to draw to them many other points. In fig. 42, C is an obvious example. We can call these collector points, junctions, nodes or sinks. They seem to attract other points. Other points feed into these collector points. In the example we have been using, item C is CANNOT SLEEP. It is immediately obvious that this is the central item and the key cause of complaint. Various other points flow into this one: LOUD NOISE, PERSISTENT, GOING ON FOR A LONG TIME, and IMPOSSIBLE TO BLOCK OUT MUSIC. At this point you might say that if you were to take a sleeping pill your problems would be solved. Less drastic would be the use of earmuffs of some sort. Collector points are important points and also possible action points. It is worth paying special attention to each collector point.

STABLE LOOPS

Every flowscape will turn out to contain at least one stable loop. This follows directly from what has been said in previous sections and also from the theorem put forward on p. 46. If you do not find a stable loop then re-examine your flowscape because it is sure to be wrong at some point.

In the flowscape shown in fig. 42, the stable loop is given by F–G–E. This is the endless repeating loop that we have met before. This gives stability to the perception. This loop which indicates that the neighbour is aggressive, dismissive and unimpressed by threats is the key area for action. Each of the points in the loop can be examined. If the neighbour is dismissive, E, then perhaps legal action could be tried: this would be more difficult to dismiss. On the other hand the aggressiveness of the neighbour, G, might be softened by a different, peace-making approach. Perhaps the very first approach was too complaining and has set up the aggression. Since threats do not work, F, you might try reciprocation by playing your own music as loudly.

LINKS

In the flowscape shown in fig. 42, H is a vital link between the collector point and the stable state. So we look more closely at H. This indicates that one of the points of weakness is that no one else is involved. There cannot be a pressure group or multiple complaints. Perhaps something could be done about this. Perhaps a neighbourhood association could be set up. This association would then be able to deal with all neighbourhood complaints – including this loud music complaint. The music-producing neighbour would either be a member of the neighbourhood association and would have to explain why the music needed to be so loud, or if not a member, then the whole association could now put pressure on him (or her).

So we see that once we have the visible flowscape in front of us we can get to work on it. We can see both the sensitive point and the important points. We can focus our attention and decide where it is best to take action. We may still have to figure out the action but figuring out focused action is much easier than deciding on vague action.

FURTHER EXAMPLES

We can now proceed to look at some further examples. In each case I want to emphasize that these are genuine stream of consciousness lists. I have not in any way contrived the examples to make a point. You can, if you wish, take the same list and make your own connexions and flowscape. Or you can start with the subject area and put together your own stream of consciousness list.

A lot of people get concerned about whether their list is comprehensive enough or whether they have made the 'right' connexions. This does not matter so much. The flowscape is a picture of your perceptions at the moment. There could be other pictures, just as walking around a house can give different perspectives. Also your perceptions may be different under different circumstances. Water logic is not a matter of being right but of flow. So proceed with the flowscape without worrying too much about getting it right.

SUBJECT

You have a faithful and loyal secretary who has worked hard for you over the years. She is getting older and the work is getting too much for her. She has not yet reached retiring age and she is unwilling to take early retirement.

LIST

A   BEEN WITH YOU MANY YEARS AND
       LOYAL   *I*

B   DOES NOT WANT TO RETIRE   *E*

C   THERE IS A NEED FOR A NEW PERSON   *F*

D   MONEY IS NO PROBLEM   *B*

E   TURF AND TERRITORY IS A PROBLEM   *B*

F   DIFFICULT TO INDICATE
      INADEQUACY   *G*

G   SECRETARY IS A SENSITIVE PERSON   *I*

H   IT HAS TO HAPPEN SOMETIME   *C*

I   EFFECT ON MORALE ELSEWHERE   *B*

J   HINTS HAVE BEEN IGNORED AND
      REJECTED   *B*

FLOWSCAPE

You can draw out your own flowscape from the flows
given in the list or you can look at the flowscape shown in
fig. 43.

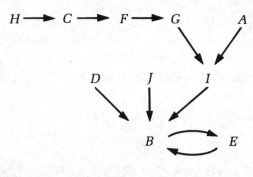

Fig. 43

We can now proceed to examine the flowscape.

Point B
This is an obvious collector point. The secretary simply
does not wish to retire. To sack her would be both
ungrateful for her loyal services and would affect morale
elsewhere.

Point I
This is also a collector point which collects up some other
feeders and then feeds them into B. In essence, I affirms
that sacking is not an option.

Chain H–C–F–G
The need for a change indicated by this chain is eventually
blocked by the impossibility of retiring the secretary
against her will.

Loop B–E

This is the stable loop and it is a very simple one. The secretary does not want to retire and does not want to give up her territory or turf. So there is no possibility of moving her to a different position. The solution might be to promote her and to have other people working under her. This way she gets to keep the turf but the work with which she cannot cope does get done by new people.

The flowscape also indicates that working on points *D* and *J* is not going to make much difference.

SUBJECT

There is the beginning of a petrol pump price war. A nearby petrol station has lowered its prices in order to get a bigger share of the business.

LIST

A   SAME CUSTOMERS   G

B   SAME PETROL   G

C   PRICE REDUCTION   G

D   MORE CUSTOMERS   G

E   LOW PROFITS   F

F   NOT SUSTAINABLE   *H*

G   COMPETITIVE EDGE   *D*

H   BOTH LOSE   *F*

I   INITIAL ADVANTAGE   *D*

J   MOTORISTS' PERCEPTION   *D*

It is interesting to note that in this list the items are put down in a rather stark manner.

FLOWSCAPE

The flowscape arising from this list is shown in fig. 44.

In examing the flowscape we might note that this time there are two quite separate organizations. One is based on the stable loop *G–D* and the other on the stable loop *F–H*.

Loop F–H
This is the direct business loop. The profits are going to be low so the price reduction is not sustainable. If you lower prices to match the competitor then both are going to suffer.

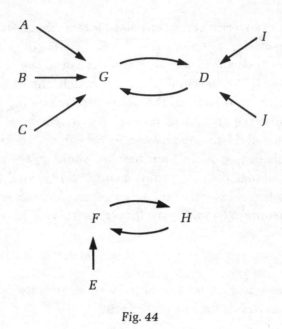

Fig. 44

Loop G–D
This is the direct marketing loop. With the lower prices
you get a competitive edge and attract more customers. It
is to be hoped that they will remain with you when you
have to raise the price eventually. This is actually your
perception of what your competitor is trying to do.

So the first point of importance is the apparent separa-
tion of the business loop from the marketing loop. One
can imagine a marketing manager arguing with a business
manager at this point.

Point G
This is a powerful collector point. Several things feed into
this desire for a COMPETITIVE EDGE. If G can be
attacked then the whole operation is pointless. If you do
immediately lower your prices to match the competitor
then there is no point in the competitor persisting or even
trying it in the first place. If, however, your competitor has
more financial backing and can go on longer at a loss then
you could be in trouble. Your best bet would still be to lower
prices but to make your profits on other things such as food
sales, other sales, different types of service, car servicing
and washing. You may have to treat petrol as a loss leader.

SUBJECT

In some countries, for example Sweden, absenteeism from
work can run as high as 25 per cent.

LIST

A   LACK OF MOTIVATION   *B*

B   AN ESTABLISHED HABIT OR CUSTOM   *D*

C   BOTH SPOUSES ARE WORKING   *E*

D   PROTECTION FROM DISMISSAL   *B*

E   THINGS TO BE DONE AT HOME, FAMILY,
      ETC.   *G*

F   FELLOW WORKERS COVER   J

G   LONG TRAVEL DISTANCE TO WORK   B

H   HIGH INCOME TAX   A

I   OTHER HOBBIES AND INTERESTS   B

J   NO SENSE OF RESPONSIBILITY   A

FLOWSCAPE

The flowscape from this list is shown in fig. 45. As before, we can examine the flowscape.

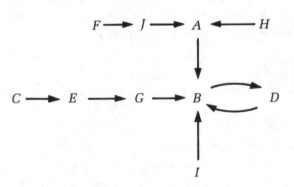

Fig. 45

Point B
This is the obvious collector point. Whatever the contributing causes the habit is now established. Workers come to expect a degree of absenteeism as part of their work style. This may suggest learning to live with it and even formalizing it. Perhaps workers could be allowed a certain number of 'absentee' days a year. Another approach might be to suggest that absentee days need to be signalled in advance. This last suggestion might not work because home and family emergencies cannot be known in advance. A further option is to allow a formally shortened working time, with permitted absentee days, but with a reduction in wages at the same time. Perhaps workers could opt for this alternative work style.

Point A
This is also a collector point and is concerned with worker motivation. If people are bored in their jobs and not motivated then they might be more casual about absenteeism. There is a great deal of work being done today throughout the world to try to raise motivation.

Chain C–E–G
Not too much can be done about these items.

Loop B–D
This is a very simple loop. There is no fear of dismissal because of union pressure and indeed job protection under the law. This is what has permitted the custom to become established. It is very unlikely that job protection can be altered in the short term. There is no fear of dismissal, but could there be other fears? Perhaps if there were some

sense of group belonging, group benefits or group penalties, then peer pressure would substitute for fear of dismissal. Perhaps work groups with the lowest absentee rate could get some privileges. Possibly, long-term workers would be more susceptible to peer and group pressure than short-term workers, who might not care too much.

SUBJECT

Sectarian or ethnic violence where two communities that live together cannot get on with each other.

LIST

A   VIOLENCE   *B*

B   REVENGE FOR PAST EVENTS   *C*

C   NEVER GIVE IN   *H*

D   ECONOMIC HARDSHIP   *J*

E   GROUP AND PEER PRESSURES   *C*

F   ANGER   *B*

G   DESPAIR   *B*

H   LABELLED AS A TRAITOR   B

I   LOCAL HEROES   C

J   THE FUTURE   D

K   SETTLEMENT   C

FLOWSCAPE

The flowscape arising from this list is shown in fig. 46. As before, we can examine this flowscape.

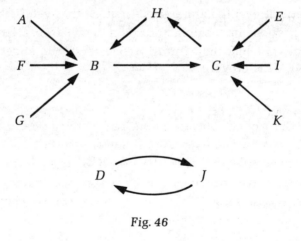

Fig. 46

Loop D–J
The first important point is that there are two separate
organizations around two stable loops. There is the small
D–J loop on its own. This suggests that economic hardship
and the future do not appear to figure largely in considerations and do not have much effect on reducing the sectarian violence. In the outer world it may well be true that
economic hardship has been a major causal factor of the
unrest but that does not mean that it figures in the
ongoing process. This illustrates quite nicely the difference
between causal analysis and the flow analysis of perception. People do not seem to refrain from sectarian violence
because it is wrecking the economy.

Point B
This is one of the two main collector clusters. The need to
avenge past events is one of the factors that keeps things
going. It seems impossible to draw a line or forget. Human
nature is not like that. Into this feed violence, anger and
despair.

Point C
This is the second collector point. This is the determination
to never give in and especially to never give in to violence
or pressure. Into this feed the power of peer and group
pressure. It also provides the base for local heroes and
leaders. It also means that any settlement must never be
seen as anybody having given in.

Loop B–C–H
This is the stabilizing loop that links both clusters. The
key link here is H. The powerful fear of being labelled as

a traitor prevents anyone from making conciliatory moves. Even if they were to make such moves they would not be effective because the traitor label would instantly remove that person from a leadership role in the group.

Not surprisingly the situation is very stable.

INNER AND OUTER WORLD

At several points in this book, and also in this section, I have made clear that water logic and flowscapes are primarily directed at the inner world of perception. In some of the examples given it may seem that the flowscape was actually describing the outer world of reality. There will be times when the two worlds do get close. If your perception describes fairly accurately what is happening in the outer world then the resemblance will be close. If the outer world is itself only determined by perceptions (how the people involved perceive things) then the resemblance will be close. Nevertheless, it is important to keep in mind that the flowscape describes perception. It is never a matter of having to 'prove a cause' or to 'offer evidence for a relationship' as it would be in an analysis of the outer world. If a relationship exists in a perception then it exists. It may be faulty or unjustified but that is irrelevant: it exists as a perception. With a flowscape we need to see its existence. Once we can see the flowscape then we can challenge or seek to alter a relationship, but that is a later step. So when you look at someone else's flowscape you should never say: 'Why do you say that?' People are beautiful and people are less beautiful, that is the reality. Some perceptions are wise and justified. Some perceptions are inadequate and biased. In a flowscape we want to see the perceptions as they are – not what we would like them to be.

This is a very important point and it can be quite difficult to grasp for those who believe they are involved in objective analysis. Usually such analysis is really no more objective but consists also of perceptions – but perceptions that can be defended by argument. It is never necessary to argue about a flowscape. You may indeed ask for elaboration or clarification if you do not understand one of the items on the base list, but that is a different matter.

It is very likely that readers tackling the sample subjects I have used here would come up with very different flowscapes. They would be just as valid as mine. Each flowscape can then be examined to see what considerations it may give rise to.

PRACTICAL TECHNIQUE

The flowscape technique shown here is a practical technique that can be learned, practised and used. It arises directly from water logic and is a practical way of using water logic. The technique can be taken and used into the future, long after the contents of the book have been forgotten. It has always been my intention to design practical processes which can then demonstrate their own value. The purpose of any conceptual model is to provide something useful. Otherwise models remain mere description and one description is as good as another.

This attitude also springs from water logic and pragmatism. I often get sent complicated descriptions of the universe and other matters. If you set your mind to it you can describe anything in a large number of different ways. Then what? What practical outcome does the description lead to? It may lead to experiments and new approaches to discovering something. Or it may lead directly to practical outcomes such as a new tool for thinking.

STREAM OF CONSCIOUSNESS – BASE LIST

The stream of consciousness list is the basis of the flow-scape. From time to time I shall refer to it as the 'base list' mainly because this is less of a mouthful than stream of consciousness and I am reluctant to create the jargon term SOC-list.

The second lesson of the CoRT* programme for the direct teaching of thinking in schools is called CAF and is pronounced 'caff'. This stands for Consider All Factors. The abbreviation is deliberate and necessary because CAF is learned and practised as a specific thinking tool and therefore requires its own identity. CAF is an encouragement to a person to consider all the factors you need to think about when focusing upon any particular situation. This process is very similar to the construction of the base list. In this base list we put down 'factors' and 'considerations'.

If you were to do a CAF on the choice of a pet your list might include:

SIZE

AMOUNT OF FOOD NEEDED

* The programme I developed for the direct teaching of thinking as a school subject.

EXERCISE NEEDED

NOISE

SPACE

PRICE

If you were to do a flowscape on the choice of a pet it would look quite similar. The base list includes items, aspects, features, things that come to mind, priorities, constraints, objectives, etc. This may seem very wide because it is meant to be very wide. It may also seem messy and vague to bundle together things like constraints and objectives. But perception is like that. The brain does not have boxes with labels on them. That is why it is called a stream of consciousness list. You put down things as they occur to you. With practice your base lists will become better and better – as a reflection of your perception.

I want to emphasize as strongly as I can that the stream of consciousness list is *not* an *analysis* of the situation. I emphasize this because people are very used to being analytical. Analysis proceeds by slicing something up and then slicing the slices up, and so on. This has its place and its merits but it is too restricting for the flowscape process. Contrast an analysis of the food requirements for a dinner party with a stream of consciousness list:

Analysis

INGREDIENTS

COOKING SKILL AVAILABLE

COOKING TIME

PREFERENCES AND ALLERGIES OF GUESTS

PRESENTATION OF FOOD

BACK-UP PLANS

Stream of Consciousness

SURPRISE

FOOD TO TALK ABOUT

FOOD TO REMEMBER

FOOD TO BE EATEN SLOWLY

PEOPLE ON DIETS

TRY SOMETHING NEW

Now it is quite true that an analyst would claim that all these items on the stream of consciousness list might eventually appear in a very comprehensive analysis. The analysis would have to be very detailed indeed for this to happen. Conversely many of the items on the analysis list could certainly appear on the stream of consciousness list.

The important point to remember is that the stream of consciousness list is not meant to be an analysis list.

The stream of consciousness or base list does not have to be comprehensive. If it had to be comprehensive it would be far too large and unwieldy. Why does it not matter if the base list is not comprehensive? Perception itself is never comprehensive. We look at things from one perspective. Our attention flows over certain features but not over others.

Fig. 47 shows a chain extending from A to D. If you were to put down just A and D you would get the same effect. It is a bit like a hologram. In a hologram all the picture is included in each part. Similarly, in perception the whole has an effect on the smaller part so whatever part we put down has been influenced by the whole.

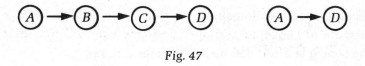

Fig. 47

In the flowscape examples we have considered so far there have been ten items on the base list. This seems very few. And yet we can get useful flowscapes even with so few items. Later we shall look at some flowscapes with twenty items on the base list.

As you get better at the flowscape technique you will start putting down on the base list items which cover several other things. For example if you were doing a base list on a grocery store your base list would not be:

ORANGES

LEMONS

APPLES

GRAPEFRUIT

MELONS

PEARS

All these items might come under FRESH FRUIT or
under an even broader heading, FRESH PRODUCE. That
would leave space on your base list for such things as
SERVICE, ATTITUDE, PRICE, etc.

In fact the base list tends to be set at a concept level
though it can still include specific items. If you have a
mixture of concepts and specific items you will find that
the concepts often end up as collector points.

The items on the base list are usually nouns or short
phrases. It would be unusual to have verbs on their own.
There would be no point in having adjectives or adverbs.
These are best converted into the related noun. For exam-
ple, in a base list on education we might have WANTING
TO LEARN or, more simply, STUDENT MOTIVATION.
Sometimes, however, phrases are more graphic than static
descriptions. For example, the phrase CANNOT BE
BOTHERED is more powerful than DISINTEREST.

Even though it is so easy, putting down the base list
improves with practice. The items put on the list are more
comprehensive and more significant. But you should not
try to do this consciously. You just put down what comes
into your head. A base list on locating a shop might be:

WHICH SIDE DO PEOPLE WALK ON

NEAR A BUS STOP

ABILITY TO PARK

SIMILAR SHOPS HELP

SIMILAR SHOPS DO NOT HELP (COMPETE)

VISIBLE FROM A PASSING CAR

PRICE OF SHOP (OR SITE)

PRICE OR QUALITY OF GOODS TO BE SOLD

This base list contains a contradiction. Similar shops nearby might act as competition and take custom away from you. On the other hand, similar shops nearby might attract to that area shoppers looking for a certain type of goods. As I have said before, there are no contradictions in perception. You just put down both items on the base list.

You may find it quite difficult to put down even ten items on a base list, let alone twenty items. If you find it quite easy and if you find that you have far too many items that you want to put down, it is possible that you are working at the detail level (like the oranges, lemons, apples in the grocer). If this is the case then just put down all the items you want, no matter how long the list might be. Then you look at the whole list and try to reduce it to a manageable size (ten or twenty items) by combining different items together. For example, the initial base list for education might include:

GIFTED CHILDREN

CATERING FOR SPECIAL NEEDS

ADVANCED INSTRUCTION

NURTURING TALENT

All these items might be put together under:

SPECIAL NEEDS OF GIFTED CHILDREN

If there were a need to explore this particular area itself then a flowscape could be done on this subject in its own right.

PROBLEM SOLVING

The flowscape is not directly a problem-solving technique. What I mean is that once we have the flowscape we can then proceed to use this as a basis for problem solving as I illustrated in many of the examples of flowscapes. The danger is that if you set out to use the flowscape as a problem-solving tool then the items you put down on the base list will not reflect your perception of the situation itself but only *what you wish to do*. This is very limiting. So it is far more effective to do a flowscape on the situation itself – and then to use this flowscape as a basis for problem solving. Such problem solving may use the sort of methods which I used with the examples but it can also use direct methods of intervention, which will be

described in the later section that is concerned with altering flowscapes.

It is always possible to do a flowscape on your approach
to the problem, or even on the traditional approach. This
will give a picture of the existing approach and this can
be the basis for suggesting new approaches.

MORE COMPLEX FLOWSCAPES

The purpose of setting up a flowscape is to look at it. You should be able to look at a flowscape much as a geographer, farmer or developer looks at a landscape: noting; commenting; seeing points of interest; seeing points of significance; picking out points for action; and generally deciding where attention is best focused.

If people are going to give this sort of serious attention to a flowscape they usually want to know if it is 'right'. It is well known that a complex mathematical model of an economic situation is quite useless if one of the links is incorrect or something has been left out. Since the creation of a flowscape seems so easy these doubts about it being 'right' can be strong.

I repeat here what I have written at several points in this book. The world of water logic and flowscapes is different from the world of rock logic, judgement, boxes and 'it is right'.

Flowscapes are really quite robust and changes at one point may have little impact on the whole. I shall illustrate this point with the next flowscape example.

SUBJECT

Choosing a holiday.

LIST

A   COST   I

B   CLIMATE   Q

C   LOW HASSLE   Q

D   GOOD COMPANY   G

E   ACTIVITIES   T

F   SIGHTSEEING   E

G   RELAXING   T

H   SOMETHING TO TALK ABOUT   R

I   AGREEMENT OF ALL PARTIES   H

J   EXPERIENCE   K

K   PRIOR KNOWLEDGE   E

L   TOLERANCE   O

M   PLAN AHEAD   P

N   ADVICE   K

O   RISK   A

P   TIME OF YEAR   B

Q   INTERESTS   G

R   ANTICIPATION   Q

S   HEALTH   T

T   ENERGY   Q

FLOWSCAPE

The first step in laying out the flowscape is to look down the letters of the alphabet on the right hand side (the destination letters). See which letter occurs most often and put that down. Next connect up all the letters that flow to that point. The result is shown in fig. 49. This

forms the core around which the flowscape can now be
built.

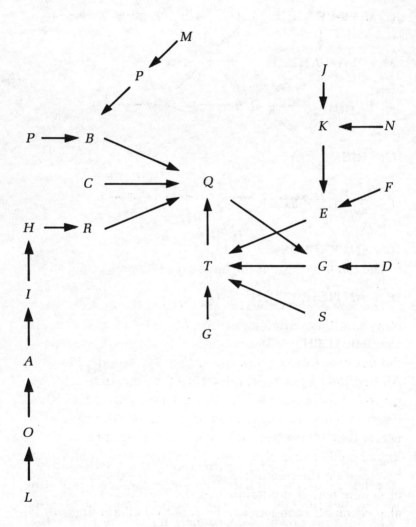

Fig. 48

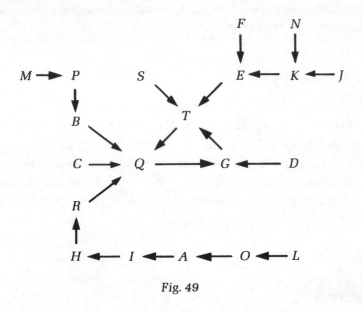

Fig. 49

The full first draft of the flowscape is shown in fig. 48.

The first draft is always rather messy. Lines cross each other and there are long arrows of connection. We might also note that there are two mistakes in this flowscape. I did not insert these on purpose, they did actually happen. All the flowscapes used in this book are genuine and not contrived for a purpose. You may notice that P has been inserted twice and in each case goes to B. You may also notice that G has been inserted twice in its link with T. You should always check out a flowscape after completion by counting the number of letters put down, which must of course match the number in the base list. You should also check off each letter to be sure that all are present. If all letters are present and the number is correct then your flowscape is probably correct even though you may still have put the wrong arrows.

EXAMINATION

If we were to go back to the base list we might wonder whether G, which represents RELAXING, might not just as easily have flowed to C, LOW HASSLE, or to Q, INTERESTS. If we try out these substitutions on the actual flowscape we see that the stable loop has shifted but everything else is much the same. This is what I mean by the stability of flowscapes.

Point Q
This is obviously a key collector point. The term INTER-ESTS may seem rather broad and impersonal. This is quite true and in individual cases it would be more useful to spell out actual interests.

Point G
This is an important point because the important collector point Q leads into it. The term RELAXING may seem rather inadequate at this point. The broader term 'enjoyment' might have been better but there is a great danger in using terms as broad as 'enjoyment' on the base list. The danger is that the whole flowscape will then flow into 'enjoyment' and the flowscape will simply state the obvious: 'the best choice for a holiday is an enjoyable holiday'.

Chain L–O–A–I–H–R
This long chain feeds into Q. All the items in the chain

feed one into the other almost as 'attributes' needed for the right choice. Surprisingly COST and AGREEMENT are not seen as collector points.

Loop Q–G–T
This suggests that the key elements are that the holiday should be relaxing and should match the interests and energy levels of the group.

As always, flowscapes, having to do with perception, are very individual. Another person might have put even more emphasis on *D*, GOOD COMPANY, which is important as it feeds directly into *G*.

SUBJECT

Choosing a career.

LIST

The stream of consciousness or base list given here is somewhat abstract and is based on conversations with young people at that stage in their lives.

A   QUALITY OF LIFE   *B*

B   QUALIFICATIONS   *I*

C   INCOME   *A*

D   LOCATION   *A*

E   SOCIAL STATUS   *G*

F   PROSPECTS OF ADVANCEMENT   *C*

G   SELF-IMAGE   *A*

H   THE PEOPLE AROUND   *A*

I   INTERESTING   *A*

J   POSSIBILITY OF SELF-EXPRESSION   *I*

K   ECONOMIC CLIMATE   *F*

L   FAMILY LIFE   *A*

M   BASE FOR OTHER THINGS   *O*

N   GOOD FOR CURRICULUM VITAE   *O*

O   POSSIBILITY OF CHANGE LATER   *F*

P   AMOUNT OF HARD WORK INVOLVED   *Q*

Q   HEALTH FACTORS   *A*

R   BOREDOM   *A*

S   TIME FACTOR   *M*

T   PENSION PLANS   *A*

U   HOLIDAYS   *A*

FLOWSCAPE

The flowscape is shown in fig. 50. As usual, we can examine the flowscape.

Point A
This is so powerful a collector point that we have to wonder if the concept is not just too broad. Does it mean only: 'the right job is the job that is best for me'? As I indicated with the previous flowscape example, such a very broad concept is not much use. The interesting contrast is between *A* and *C*, which is also a collector point.

Point C
The input from *S–M–N–O–K–F* all ends up feeding into *C*, which is hardly surprising since *C* is INCOME. At one time, or for some people, income would be the major collector point. In the past it was usual to set out to earn a good income and then that would pay for the 'quality of life' that was desired. Today young people are more

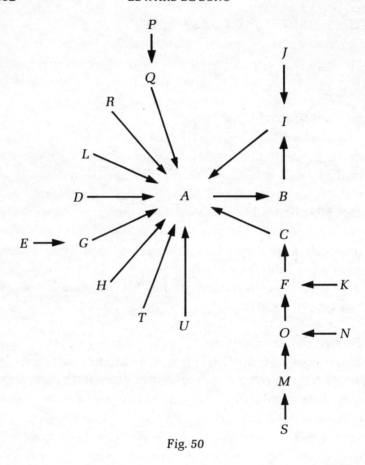

Fig. 50

inclined to ask whether there is much point in spending a life earning money without the possibility of translating this into a quality of life.

Point F
This point is important because it includes not only advancement in the present job but also the possibilities of a change in career.

Loop A–B–I
This seems a stable and sensible loop: the job that satisfies interests, provides the needed quality of life and also fits the qualifications of the candidate. Income is not directly in the loop but is a contribution to the quality of life.

In a sense this particular flowscape is a bit predictable and a bit dull and contains no surprises. Perhaps the dominance of quality of life over income is stronger than might be expected. There will be many times when flowscapes turn out to be no more than summaries of what we already know or feel. In this case we may wish to go further and do a specific flowscape on 'Quality of life' to explore the perceptions around that.

SUBJECT

Around the world there is great concern with rapidly escalating health care costs. The rise in these costs greatly exceeds the rise in GNP or even inflation. The flowscape is on the general subject of 'Health care costs' and is not a problem-solving exercise as such.

LIST

A   ADVANCES IN TECHNOLOGY   *B*

B   MEDICAL SCIENCE CAN DO MORE AND
      MORE   *D*

C   PUBLIC EXPECTATIONS ARE ALWAYS
     INCREASING   D

D   DEMAND FOR HEALTH CARE   F

E   PERSONNEL COSTS   Q

F   HEROIC MEDICINE   G

G   LIFE AT ANY COST   O

H   POLITICAL FOOTBALL   R

I   MALPRACTICE INSURANCE   T

J   PEOPLE LIVE LONGER   K

K   CHRONIC SICK   G

L   COMMERCIAL DRUG SALES   Q

M   HEALTH CONSCIOUSNESS   C

N   NO PLACE AT HOME   D

O   HIGH COST OF LAST MONTH OF LIFE   F

P   COST OF TESTS   B

Q   NO ECONOMIC CONSTRAINTS   G

R   NO RESTRAINT MECHANISM   H

S   DUTY OF RELATIVES   G

T   DOCTORS' FEES   E

There are many other factors that might have been put on the list. Items on the list might also have been expressed differently. You can repeat the exercise with your own list.

FLOWSCAPE

The resulting flowscape is shown in fig. 51. The first obvious point of interest is that there are two loops: a large loop and a very small one.

Loop H–R
This separate loop simply indicates that there is no restraining mechanism and that this is a political football. No politician dare suggest the restriction of health services where these are provided by the state because that would be an instant loss of votes. In a free enterprise country like the USA, there can be an attempt to bring down costs of the privately offered health care but any attempt to

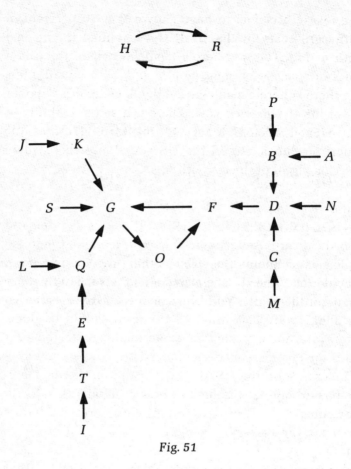

Fig. 51

curtail it would meet stiff opposition. Although this loop seems too small, in the end it may be the more important loop.

Loop F–G–O
The loop involves heroic medicine, the notion that life must be preserved at any cost, and the last month of life.

Some research claims to have shown that 70 per cent of health care costs in the USA are sustained in the last month of life. There is heroic medicine where there is a chance of recovery or some months of a better quality life. Then there is heroic medicine simply to get another day or hour of life at whatever cost. There is also the inability of relatives and doctors to accept the turning off of life support machines, etc. In the USA, and elsewhere, there are serious legal problems with this.

Point D

This is a powerful collector point. It covers the demand for medical care. As technology can do more and more so people's expectations rise. If something can be done then it should be done. If one person has a successful liver transplant then this should be provided if it seems necessary. If there are tests then all the tests should be done. Doctors are not expected to make mistakes so they get sued if mistakes are made. This leads to rises in malpractice insurance (in the USA). The demand for 'heroic medicine' or medicine at the limits of its possibilities is likely to continue.

Point Q

This is another collector point which simply states that there is NO RESTRAINT MECHANISM. Price is not itself a restraint because relatives feel they must pay the price whatever it may be. Total cost to the government is not a restraint because if you or your child is ill then aggregate costs mean nothing.

The guilt and duty factor, S, is important because it

leads to LIFE AT ANY COST, G. If there was an accept-
ance of death and a removal of the guilt aspect then the
flowscape might look rather different. If we create the
concept of SENSIBLE MEDICINE, X, then the flowscape
might change to the one (relevant part only) shown in fig.
52. This shows the opening up of the F–G–O loop and the
creation of a new loop S–X. The relatives still have their
sense of duty and obligation but it can now be discharged,
without guilt, through the new concept of SENSIBLE
MEDICINE.

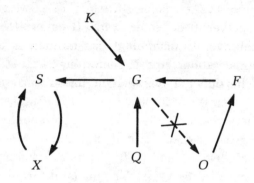

Fig. 52

This introduction of a new concept is an example of the
sort of intervention it is possible to make to alter the flow
of a flowscape. Interventions of this sort will be dealt
with in detail in a later section.

COMPLEXITY

There is no fundamental difference between a simple
flowscape (ten list points) and a more complex flowscape

(twenty or more list points). The mechanics are the same. The only advantage of the larger size of list is that you can put down more points when the situation itself is complex. In the end there will be stable loops, collector points and feeder chains as before. It is quite likely that larger lists will split into two or more organizations around separate stable loops.

It is always possible to analyse a subject, to divide it into sub-subjects and construct a flowscape on each of these. There is then some difficulty in putting the flowscapes together. It is better to make a complex flowscape to give the overall picture. At this point it is possible to put together further flowscapes on elements of the larger picture. This way the overall structure is set up first.

CONCEPTS

Legal documents often contain paragraphs like, 'The house at number 14 Belmont Road, the house at number 41 Cornwall Avenue and the house at number 12 Drake Street comprise the property hereinafter referred to as The Property.' So instead of listing the different houses each time they are referred to, it is only necessary to write 'The Property'.

A concept is a similar package of convenience which puts a number of things together so that they can be referred to as a whole. In a sense every word is a concept. There is a concept of a mountain which is referred to by that word. There is the concept of justice which includes fair play, moral values and the administration of the law. Obviously it is easier to be certain about what goes into a concept where the subject is physical and can be observed than when it is abstract. A great deal of classic Greek thinking and Socratic dialogue went into discussing and arguing about what actually should go into concepts such as justice.

So there are concepts which have been crystallized into words: crime, justice, punishment, mercy, etc. Then there are packages for which we do not yet have a word. This may be because it is but a temporary package (as with the legal document) or because language is quite slow at creating and admitting new words. We could call these 'naked' concepts since they are like a crab without the hard shell of a word around them. Such naked concepts have to be described by a phrase, a combination of other words.

All the stream of consciousness lists given in this book contain a variety of concepts. These may be well established concepts like COST or SOCIAL STATUS. There are also less established concepts such as LOW HASSLE and HEROIC MEDICINE. There may even be more complicated concepts like HIGH COST OF LAST MONTH OF LIFE. This last example is on the borderline between a described factor and a concept.

As I have indicated there is some danger if the concepts we use in the base list are too broad. For example, in the flowscape on 'Choosing a holiday' if we had inserted the concept ENJOYABLE we might have ended up with showing that the best way to choose a holiday was to choose an enjoyable holiday. This is like saying the best holiday is the best one to choose. The same consideration applied to 'Choosing a career'. If we had inserted the concept SUITS ME BEST we would have arrived at the conclusion that the best career was the one which suits a person best. Since this is just a repeat of the question it has little practical value.

For the base lists we need to put in concepts that are broad enough to cover a lot of detail but not so broad that they just repeat the question: 'How would you solve this problem?'

'With the appropriate answer.'

In addition to using concepts for the base list we can also extract concepts from the flowscape when we have it before us. Any major collector point is automatically a useful concept which may, or may not, be adequately described by the item on the base list. For example, in 'Choosing a holiday' the point INTERESTS is a major collector point. We may leave this as it is or redefine it.

Sometimes a whole loop can become a concept. For example, in the 'Health care costs' flowscape the whole stable loop could be characterized as 'the need to strive to maintain life at any cost'. This is not quite the same as heroic medicine, though this comes into it. The concept of 'health as a right' is produced by a combination of demands, expectations and lack of economic considerations.

One of the main benefits of examining flowscapes is to realize how powerful certain clusterings of factors might be. This can be a moment of insight. For convenience we may wish to create a concept to represent such clusterings.

CONCEPTS, CATEGORIES AND ARISTOTLE

It was Aristotle's great contribution to create rock logic. This was done by forming the idea of 'categories'. These could be clearly defined. For example there might be a category (or concept) of a 'dog'. When you encountered an animal you would judge whether it belonged in that category or not. If it did belong then we might say or think, 'This is a dog.' Once we had made that judgement then we could ascribe all the characteristics of the dog category to the creature. For example we might expect the creature to bark and behave like a dog. Since 'this is a dog' and 'this is not a dog' could not both be right we got the principle of contradiction – which is the basis of the logic.

There is nothing wrong with concepts and categories as exploratory devices. It is when they are used for the rigid arguments of rock logic that there may be trouble. Using water logic or flow notation, the benefits of having concepts and categories are shown in fig. 53.

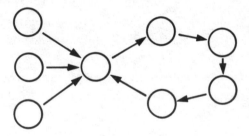

Fig. 53

Here we can see how the different attributes feed into the collector point of the concept. From the concept we then get a loop consisting of all the fixed characteristics of that concept. It is fairly easy to see that the whole thing is either a guessing game or circular. If a creature has all the attributes of a dog then we can call it a dog, but doing so will not provide anything we do not know already. If

the creature has only some of the attributes then we can
call it a dog and it will now get the rest of the attributes.
This is a guessing game because we assume that a creature
cannot have some of the attributes of a dog and not the
others – just as a duckbilled platypus has a bill like a
duck but has fur and four legs.

In practice the process is more as shown in fig. 54. Here
the hints or clues suggest a hypothesis or guess. This guess
is then checked out by looking for vital features. If the check
is passed then the concept description can be applied.

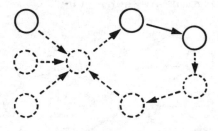

Fig. 54

LUMPING AND SPLITTING

Science has always been a matter of lumping together into
a single concept things which may seem different, and
separating into two concepts things which seem the same.
Fig. 55 shows part of a flowscape in which two collector
points are linked together by a single name, *N-1*. A scien-
tist now spots a vital X factor. One of the groups has this
X factor and the other does not. The flowscape now splits

into two, as shown in fig. 56, and this split is stabilized by
two new names, N-2 and N-3.

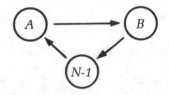

Fig. 55

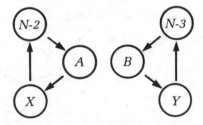

Fig. 56

This process of increased discrimination happens all
the time. That is how different diseases get identified so
that treatment can be more specific.

The same process can happen in reverse. In Australia
there is a wealth of brightly coloured parrots, parakeets,
lorikeets etc. Amongst all these there is one bird which is
almost completely red and another which is almost completely green. For a long time these were considered to be
two different species. Then it was realized that they were
just the male and female of the same species. This process of
lumping is shown in fig. 57. Two separate groupings are
united by a common feature and the grouping is stabilized

with a new name N-4, though it could retain one of the old names.

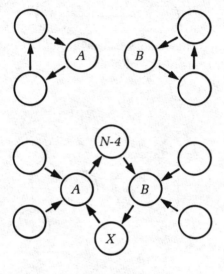

Fig. 57

CONCEPTS AND FLEXIBILITY

There was a classic experiment in which students were given some electrical components and asked to make up a circuit to ring a bell. There was not quite enough wire given to complete the circuit. Most students gave up and declared that it was impossible. A few made use of the metal shaft of the supplied screwdriver to complete the circuit. The majority of students looked for a 'piece of wire'. The exceptional students worked at a concept level and looked for a 'piece of metal'.

The ability to work at a concept level is crucial for creativity and for thinking in general. As shown in fig. 58, we need to keep moving constantly from the actual detail level to the concept level and back again. This is how we move from idea to idea. This is the basis of constructive thinking, for otherwise we are limited to experience and what is before us at the moment.

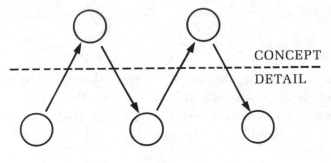

Fig. 58

Fig. 59 is an illustration of training. You can train someone to react to situation *A* with response *1*, to situation *B* with response *2*, and to situation *C* with response *3*. The training is effective and these trained people know what to do. But if, one day, situation *A* occurs and response *1* is not possible then that person will be lost.

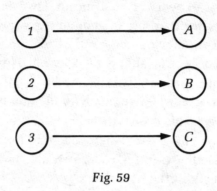

Fig. 59

But if the people had been trained using a function concept to link situation and reaction then that person might have looked around and found that another response might also carry out that function concept, as shown in fig. 60.

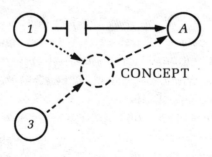

Fig. 60

That is why it might be limiting to accelerate the learning of young children. They can be taught responses but may lose out on the development of concepts.

PRE-CONCEPTS AND POST-CONCEPTS

Most concepts are convenient package descriptions after we know what is in the package. The legal paragraph used at the beginning of the section defines the relevant properties precisely. I call these post-concepts because they occur after the event. This packaging for the sake of convenience is shown in fig. 61, which also indicates how the concept is stabilized by a name.

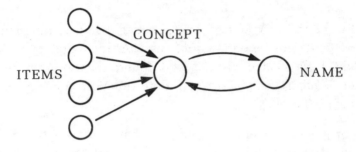

Fig. 61

Sometimes, however, we start at exactly the opposite end. We know what the concept should do but we do not know what the concept is. Any writer knows this well, as he or she searches for just the right word to describe a complex set of features. An engineer might say: 'At this point we need something that is going to change shape and to form a shape we have predetermined.' The engineer knows the features of what is wanted. The answer could be a type of memory metal which reverts back to a previous shape at a given temperature. Such metals are now in use. The process is illustrated in fig. 62. A pre-concept is like defining a hole and then looking for something to fit that hole.

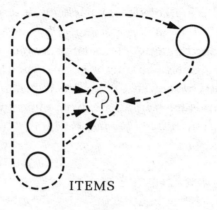

ITEMS

Fig. 62

In a post-concept we find the characteristics together and name this cluster a concept. In a pre-concept we put together the characteristics and then look around for something to fit the defined need. This is an important part of problem solving. A pre-concept is a bit like a hypothesis since it allows us to move ahead of where we are at the moment.

I sometimes distinguish between three types of question. In a 'shooting question' we know what we are aiming at and the answer is 'yes' or 'no'. This is a checking-out question. In a 'fishing question' we bait the hook and wait to see what turns up. This is an open-ended search for more information. In a 'trapping question' we prepare the trap to suit what we want to catch. This is exactly the same as a pre-concept. We define the needs and then look for a way of satisfying those needs.

BLURRY CONCEPTS

In most of our thinking we are encouraged to be precise. This is very much the nature of rock logic. In water logic, however, the concern is for movement: where do we flow to? There are times when a blurry or vague concept is actually more use than a precise concept. A blurry concept can act as a better collector point and therefore a better connector point. Which is the more useful of the following two statements? 'I need a match to light this fire' or, 'I need "some way" of lighting this fire.'

In the first case you look specifically for a match and if you do not find a match you are blocked. In the second case your search is much broader. You might use a lighter, you might take a light from a gas pilot light, you might generate a spark, and so on.

In an earlier book of mine (*Practical Thinking*, London: Penguin, 1971), I wrote about 'porridge words' and the value of blurry concepts. A precise concept may fix where we are. A blurry concept allows us to move forward. Once again, this is partly related to the 'fuzzy logic' that is now so fashionable in the computer world.

Precision often locks us into the past, what 'is' and what has been. Blurry concepts open up the future, movement and what might be. A blurry concept is not the same as sloppy thinking. A blurry concept is definite in its own way.

WORKING BACKWARDS AND
THE CONCEPT FAN

One way to solve problems is to work backwards. This is not so easy to do if we do not know the solution to the problem. If you want to reach point *P* you can work backwards from that point but if you are not sure where point *P* might be, that is not easy.

There is, however, a way of working backwards that I have called. The Concept Fan. This is described in more detail in *Serious Creativity* (New York and London: Harper Collins, 1992) but I shall also mention it here since it really depends on the flow of water logic.

Suppose the purpose of our thinking is to tackle the problem of 'Traffic congestion in cities'. From that defined purpose we work backwards. What broad concepts might help us with that problem? We might reduce the traffic load. We might improve flow on the existing road system. We might increase the available road surface. Each of these are broad concepts – there may be more.

How might we feed these broad concepts? This is the same notion as the feeding of a collector point. How might we reduce traffic? We could encourage the use of vehicles with more people on board. We could discourage drivers from coming into the city. We could reduce the need for people to come into the city. Again there will be other concepts which feed the broad concept of reducing traffic. We would do the same for each of the other broad concepts.

Next we see how we could feed these concepts. In practice this means seeing how the concepts could be put into practical operation. For example, how might we get vehicles with more people on board? By encouraging the use of public transport and making this better, encouraging car pools and sharing, giving privilege lanes to vehicles with several occupants, or by restricting central parking.

We do the same for each concept. How might we discourage drivers from driving into the city? By charging a special fee for entrance before ten in the morning (as in Singapore), making no provision for parking and using tough measures for illegal parking, publicizing pollution levels in the city, or by publicizing the actual rate of car movement in the city.

The process is shown schematically in fig. 63. At the left-hand side we end up with a number of practical ideas which feed into the concepts, which in turn feed into the broad concepts, which in turn help with the problem.

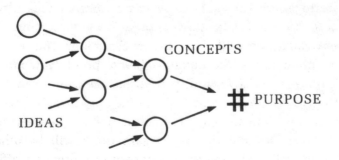

Fig. 63

The interesting point is that our search is moving backwards from the purpose (going from the right-hand side to the left-hand side) but the flow path of achievement is flowing from the left-hand side to the right-hand side.

The process can be very powerful if you are good at putting down the different concepts. This requires some practice. The concept fan is not an analysis of the situation but an elaborated flowscape.

At times you may reach a pre-concept or a defined need but not have a way of doing it. For example, you might seek to discourage drivers by 'damaging their cars'. Is it possible to find a way of doing this which would be effective but also acceptable? Possibly not.

CONCEPTS AND FLOW

This section of the book is important because concepts are a very important part of flow and water logic. Concepts are collector points or junctions. Concepts allow things to come together. Concepts allow us to move across from idea to idea. Concepts allow us to describe things but also to search for things (pre-concepts). The better you become at using concepts the better you will be at water logic. The question is always, 'Where does this take us?' rather than, 'What is this?'

INTERVENTIONS

At some points in the examination of the sample flow-scapes I have suggested interventions. For example, with the 'Health care costs' flowscape I suggested that the development of the concept of SENSIBLE MEDICINE could make a big difference to the flowscape because it would break the stable loop between HEROIC MEDI-CINE, LIFE AT ANY COST and HIGH COST OF LAST MONTH OF LIFE.

One of the purposes of laying out a flowscape is to get insight and understanding of our perceptions. Another purpose is to see if the flowscape can be changed. The flowscape gives us something tangible to work upon. Just as a road engineer examines the terrain in order to see where to build a road so we can examine the flowscape in order to see what we can do.

We now come to an interesting point. The flowscape is really a map of our perceptions, of the inner world. This may correspond to the outer world or it may not. Usually it corresponds in some parts but not in others. When we seek to change the flowscape are we seeking to change the inner world or the outer world? Are we trying to improve our perceptions or to solve real world problems? The answer is that we are usually trying to do both. The flowscape allows us to see what points might be useful to change in our perception of the outer world. If our perception does correspond to the outer world then these can become useful approaches to solving a problem. If our perception is faulty then the approaches will be of less value.

The example of the introduction of the concept of SENSIBLE MEDICINE is interesting because it works both on the inner world and also on the outer world. The notion of 'sensible medicine' in our minds and the minds of people considering the matter can change our perceptions of the problem of health care costs. That is the inner world. In the outer world, if the concept of sensible medicine was publicized and established then this might eventually lead to reduced health care costs because relatives would no longer feel guilty about not trying everything possible.

In order to consider some aspects of intervention we can set up a specific flowscape to work upon.

SUBJECT

Juvenile crime.

LIST

A   GANGS   G

B   TV CULTURE   J

C BOREDOM O

D CONSUMER PRESSURE J

E INABILITY TO EARN D

F LACK OF SKILLS E

G PEER PRESSURE J

H EXCITEMENT O

I DRUG NEEDS E

J NO INHIBITIONS H

K NO FEARS J

L PARENTS' NEEDS D

M NOTHING TO LOSE J

N DRAB SURROUNDINGS P

O ADVENTURE J

P   SCHOOL DROP-OUTS   E

Q   LOW EXPECTATIONS   E

R   ROLE MODELS   J

S   LENIENT SENTENCES   J

FLOWSCAPE

The flowscape is shown in fig. 64.

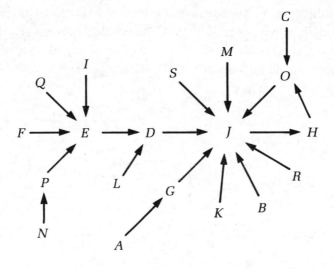

Fig. 64

Point J
This is a major collector point. The sort of insight that one
might get from this, is that lack of inhibitions is a major
factor. Most people think of crime as being something
exceptional because most people are inhibited by background, peer pressure or fear of being punished. But there
are groups where crime is not the exception but the
'culture'. That forces us to look at things in a somewhat
different way.

If crime is a culture then it needs to be tackled with
'culture weapons'. This means role models, heroes, local
values, etc. So we would seek to create or strengthen a
link between *J* and *R*. We would seek to flow from lack of
inhibitions to behaviour determined by positive role
models. If we succeeded then we would replace the stable
loop *J–H–O* with a new loop *J–R*. The changed part of the
flowscape is now shown in fig. 65.

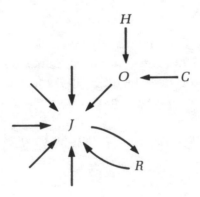

Fig. 65

This is an example of intervention. The intervention affects both how we see the situation (the inner world) and also what approach we might take (the outer world).

Loop J–H–O

This stable loop is heavily dependent on the need for excitement and adventure. This is fuelled by TV culture in two ways. The first way is in terms of the adventure models on TV. The second way is that TV makes for passive stimulation and the need for more and more stimulation.

We could use the need for excitement and adventure in a different way. For example, the Westrek Project in Western Australia takes delinquent youngsters out into the countryside and gets them involved in worthwhile projects, including special constructions, etc. There are many similar projects. We might assign the letter X to projects of this type. So now X enters the loop as shown in fig. 66.

The loop is the same but now some of the search for excitement might come not from crime but from taking part in the projects. The difficulty, of course, is funding such projects so that they have a major impact.

This is an example of intervention by insertion of a new point.

Point D

This is a major collecting point and represents the pressure on consumers to buy (ghetto blasters, sports shoes,

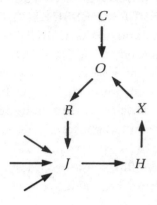

Fig. 66

local fashion gear). The main feeder is E which is itself a collector point and represents inability of youngsters to earn. In places where tourism provides a possibility for youngsters to earn in service jobs the school drop-out rate is high.

The link between E and D could be blocked or weakened by a scheme which paid youngsters for going on to higher education and perhaps even paid them according to their grades.

This is another example of a possible intervention.

Point E
This collector point is fed by factors which contribute to the youngsters' inability to earn. This probably applies more to the school-leavers than to those still at school. One of these factors is LOW EXPECTATIONS, Q. It is

well known that poverty is often as much psychological as economic. If PEER PRESSURE, G, could be used to raise expectations and if the CONSUMER PRESSURE, D, could be harnessed to PEER PRESSURE then a new loop would be formed Q–E–D–G, as shown in fig. 67a. One possible way of doing this might be to have groups formed around talented individuals to push these on and, somehow, to share in the success.

At this point the flowscape would split into two separate parts: the 'culture loop' and the 'economic loop'.

We can take another flowscape example to illustrate further interventions.

SUBJECT

There is an old church which is standing in the way of a major road development. The church is of historic value and there are those who want to preserve it. The road is necessary for the neighbourhood where employment is low and there is a need to improve the infrastructure in order to attract more business.

LIST

A   CHURCH CAN NEVER BE REBUILT   B

B   CHURCH IS PART OF HERITAGE   J

C   ROAD IS ESSENTIAL   D

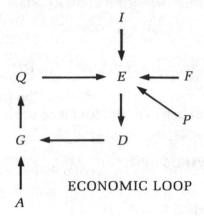

ECONOMIC LOOP

Fig. 67a

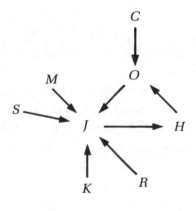

CULTURE LOOP

Fig. 67b

D   ROAD CANNOT BE PUT ELSEWHERE   E

E   LOCAL BUSINESS PRESSURE FOR
        ROAD   *C*

F   NOT MANY VISITORS TO THE CHURCH   *C*

G   LOCAL TOURIST ATTRACTION   *B*

H   ROAD WILL IMPROVE EMPLOYMENT   *E*

I   FUNDS ARE LIMITED   *D*

J   MORE VOTES IN KEEPING THE
        CHURCH   *A*

FLOWSCAPE

The flowscape is shown in fig. 68. Not surprisingly, the flowscape has divided neatly into two parts. Each part represents one particular point of view. To solve the dispute both points of view need to be brought together.

There are no contradictions in water logic so we can suppose a new concept (in fact a classic pre-concept) in which the road goes where it has to go and, at the same time, the church remains where it is. In normal logic that would be an impossible contradiction.

Fig. 69 shows this concept in place. The two separate points of view are now linked into one whole. But what is

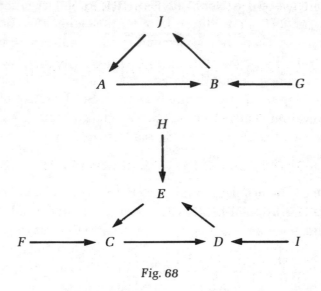

Fig. 68

the concept? We leave the church where it is and simply construct a tunnel that runs underneath the church. But there are only limited funds available. So some sort of toll is charged for use of the road until the extra costs are paid off.

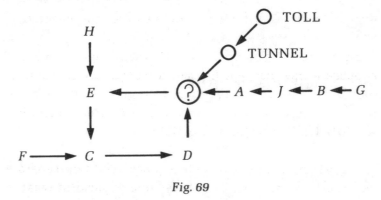

Fig. 69

Here we see a more complex type of intervention. A 'provocation' is introduced in order to see its effect on the flowscape. Then we look around to turn that provocation, impossibility or pre-concept into reality. The definition of a provocation is that there may not be a reason for saying something until after it has been said. So the effect of the provocation is tested in the flowscape and if it seems to have value then an effort is made to give reality to the provocation.

The same problem could have been approached another way. The original context was one of limited funds. We would imagine a change in that context by saying that unlimited funds were available. This might lead to the notion of moving the church (depending on its size) or the tunnel solution. Real or imagined context changes are an important aspect of intervention as we shall see in the next example.

SUBJECT

Racism.

LIST

A   INFLUENCE OF PARENTS   O

B   SCHOOLS   *F*

C   NAME-CALLING   *S*

D   BLAME FOR EVERYTHING   L

E   NEED TO HATE   D

F   US/THEM IDENTITY NEED   E

G   INCIDENTS ARE AMPLIFIED   S

H   INCIDENTS ARE PROVOKED   E

I   GOSSIP AND RUMOUR   G

J   SOMETHING TO TALK ABOUT   I

K   CROSS-GENDER ENCOURAGEMENT   E

L   SENSE OF FEAR   E

M   SENSE OF SUPERIORITY   F

N   TRADITION   O

O   EMBEDDED IN LANGUAGE/CULTURE   F

P   REASON FOR INJUSTICE AND HARSH
    TREATMENT   D

Q   PERCEIVED DIFFERENCE IN VALUES AND
     BEHAVIOUR   *F*

R   AMPLIFIED BY LEADERS   *F*

S   SELF-FULFILLING PERCEPTION   *G*

T   FEELING OF DIFFERENCE   *S*

Cross-gender encouragement means that men encourage
women and women encourage men.

FLOWSCAPE

The flowscape is shown in fig. 70. This is a flowscape that
has divided into two parts.

Loop G–S
The mind sees what it is prepared to see. In the process of
SELF-FULFILLING PERCEPTION, S, INCIDENTS
ARE AMPLIFIED and noted, G. That is a basic stabilizing
factor into which is fed GOSSIP AND RUMOUR, NAME-
CALLING and the basic FEELING OF DIFFERENCE.

Loop E–D–L
Here we have the NEED TO HATE, someone to BLAME
FOR EVERYTHING, and SENSE OF FEAR itself. The
first loop was perceptual and this second loop is emotional.

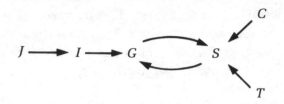

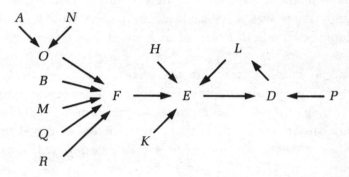

Fig. 70

Point F
This is a major collecting point with five direct feeds and two indirect feeds. Into this feed TRADITION, culture, influence on youth and the influence of leaders. So this is really the 'culture' point and here culture is meant in the broadest sense.

Point O
This is a lesser collector point and really covers the way
in which the racism is embedded in ordinary matters so
that even without focusing on it, the way of talking,
thinking and looking at the world sets racism as the
norm.

We might intervene at G by refusing to amplify incidents. There was a time when newspapers would always
identify the ethnic group of a criminal. Most responsible
newspapers have stopped this practice because it does
tend to amplify incidents and give them a racial slant
when there really is none. Perceptions are very selective
but they still need things to feed upon. The self-fulfilling
loop can be weakened at this point. It may be argued that
in the absence of news, rumour and gossip will create
worse imaginings. This is probably true for major incidents and events but not for day to day affairs.

We could intervene at F to try to weaken the US/THEM
IDENTITY habit with shared schools and cross-divide
working groups. Affirmative action as in the USA is a
step in this direction. The baleful influence of leaders who
make use of the divide to create a power base probably
needs a structural solution – for example, the notion that
you can only get elected if your support is broad based.

The general context given here is that of poor economics,
sense of fear and sense of insecurity. We can, as a provocation, change the general context to one of confidence. This
means confidence on both sides not the confidence of
superiority on one side. We can now go back through the

base list with this context in mind and make the flow connexions.

NEW CONTEXT LIST

A   INFLUENCE OF PARENTS   Q

B   SCHOOLS   J

C   NAME-CALLING   H

D   BLAME FOR EVERYTHING   M

E   NEED TO HATE   M

F   US/THEM IDENTITY NEED   J

G   INCIDENTS ARE AMPLIFIED   N

H   INCIDENTS ARE PROVOKED   N

I   GOSSIP AND RUMOUR   K

J   SOMETHING TO TALK ABOUT   C

K   CROSS-GENDER ENCOURAGEMENT   C

L   SENSE OF FEAR   R

M   SENSE OF SUPERIORITY   C

N   TRADITION   P

O   EMBEDDED IN LANGUAGE/CULTURE   N

P   REASON FOR INJUSTICE AND HARSH
      TREATMENT   N

Q   PERCEIVED DIFFERENCE IN VALUES AND
      BEHAVIOUR   F

R   AMPLIFIED BY LEADERS   D

S   SELF-FULFILLING PERCEPTION   R

T   FEELING OF DIFFERENCE   C

FLOWSCAPE

The new flowscape is shown in fig. 71.

It can be seen at once that there are major differences.
There is now one single arrangement instead of the previous split into two.

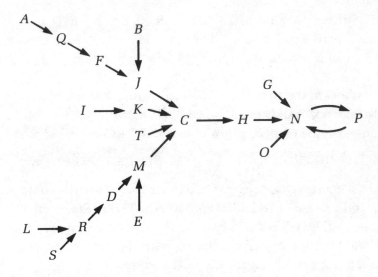

Fig. 71

Point C
This was a minor point before but now becomes a major collector point into which most things feed. This suggests that the emotional content is gone and now the difference is just a matter of being referred to by a different name. There is still a perceived difference but this is a matter of observation.

Point J
Another collector point but one without much bite. Matters which fed into F, US/THEM IDENTITY NEED, are now just things to talk about.

Point M
Much feeds into M, SENSE OF SUPERIORITY, but this only feeds into C as an extension of name calling.

Loop N–P
The items that formed the core loop before, *E–D–L*, are
now peripheral points. The new loop still indicates a
sense of tradition and a feeling of discrimination.

We can see that the differences are considerable once
the context has been changed. Racism still exists but it is
now a low-key perception rather than an emotional exercise.

Of course, this does not in any way say how the context
change is going to be brought about. The exercise merely
shows that with a context change the flowscape may be
very different. I shall be dealing with this important point
about context change in the next section.

There is a point which needs mentioning. For this
exercise I kept the stream of consciousness (or base) list
the same as before the context change. This was to show
the effect of context change on flow patterns. In practice
it might be better to start out with a new base list on
which there could be new items because the very choice of
items is influenced by the assumed or chosen context.

In many cases you may wish to make a context change
only at one particular point on the flowscape. For example,
looking at the flowscape in fig. 71 we might ask: 'Is there
any context in which *P* could flow to *C* rather than to *N*?'
We might say there could be such a context if leaders of
the groups involved suggested that it was time to stop
blaming all problems and assumed injustices on race. The
new stable loop *C–H–N–P* would be more beneficial than

the existing loop because it would suggest that the sense
of injustice was not real, but a traditional excuse.

ACTION

Problem-solving approaches and other actions can be derived from the flowscape but the flowscape itself is concerned with perception as such. It is possible to construct
a flowscape about existing actions or intended actions.
This would relate to our perception of those actions. As
usual, this may or may not fit with the outer world.

It is important to emphasize that flowscapes are about
the inner world of perception. They are not descriptions of
perception. But unless we are acting under hypnosis,
through instinct or automatically, our perceptions are the
basis of our behaviour in the outer world. Therefore the
flowscape is an important basis for action – it is not an
idle description for the sake of description.

It could even be argued that inner reality is more
important than outer reality because the inner reality of
perception determines how we see the outer world, how
we act upon the outer world and how we react to the
outer world.

Rock logic sought to escape the subjectivity of perception. Water logic seeks to explore and use the subjectivity
of perception.

CONTEXT, CONDITIONS AND
CIRCUMSTANCES

In water logic context is hugely important. I have often used the landscape or river valley analogy to illustrate the flow patterns that form in the self-organizing information system we call the brain. This analogy gives a good picture but has one major defect. The landscape is fixed and permanent. But in the brain a change of context can change the landscape. It is as if a different landscape were being observed.

Under one context or set of circumstances in the brain, state A will be succeeded by (or flow to) state B. But if the context changes then A will flow to C. The context change might be chemical. A change in the chemicals bathing the nerve cells (or released at nerve endings) will lead to different sensitivities. This is also explained in more detail in the book *I am Right — You are Wrong*. It seems likely that changes in emotion change the biochemical balance and so the flow patterns shift. This is an essential part of the functioning of the brain and not some ancient irrelevance. Self-organizing patterning systems need emotions in order to function well. Fig. 72 shows a simple flow from A to B. With a context change the flow is from A to C.

Other inputs into the brain at the same time will also alter the context because different nerve groupings will be activated or partially activated (sub-threshold). So when

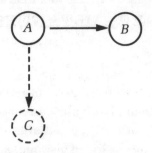

Fig. 72

the currently activated grouping (or state) tires, then a different new grouping will follow.

For this reason the basic water logic theorem is stated as follows: 'Under conditions X, state *A* will always flow to state *B*.'

We can return briefly to the jellyfish. Let us suppose that at night they disengage their stings and sting another jellyfish. There will therefore be two arrangements: the day arrangement and the night arrangement. The brain behaves in the same way but at a more complex level because there are many possible contexts.

In an argument people with opposing perceptions are often both right. Each of the opposing perceptions is based on a particular set of circumstances and context. The variability may arise in many ways.

Each party is looking at a different part of the situation.

Each party is looking at the same situation but from a different point of view (like different views of the same building).

The emotional setting is different.

Personal history and backgrounds are different.

Traditions and cultural backgrounds are different.

Immediate past history has created a different context for each of the parties.

It is characteristic of rock logic to ignore all this and to assume that the absolutes of 'truth' are independent of the current context.

Science only works because in any experiment it is assumed that the context is held constant while one factor (the experimental variable) is altered.

In some of the flowscape examples I have mentioned the huge importance of context and in one example shown the effect of a context change. For most of the examples, however, it has been assumed that the context is fixed. Is this reasonable?

The flowscape method deals with the inner world of perception. A flowscape is not a description of the outer world. Whenever a flowscape is constructed the person laying out the stream of consciousness list and making the flow connexions has some definite context in mind at that moment. So for that moment the context is fixed. If that person wishes deliberately to change the context then a different flowscape can be laid out. At a different time a new flowscape might be made and might differ from the original one because the context is different.

For this reason we do not put into a flowscape the possibility that state A can also flow to state C under different circumstances. That would not only be confusing but would be incorrect since it would refer to a possible perception, whereas flowscapes are about actual perceptions at this moment.

At the intervention stage it is now possible to speculate on how perceptions might be changed if a context were to be changed. Now we are looking at possibilities. It is always best to construct a new flowscape (or part of the flowscape) rather than to attempt to show the change on the same flowscape. This causes confusion because you can always add a new flow arrow but you cannot remove an existing one. The use of different colours is a help but it is far better to lay out a new flowscape for the new context.

What about 'if' factors? 'If he were rich this would happen ... but if he were poor then this would happen ...' 'If the sun were shining then I would do this ... if the sun were not shining I would do that ...' When you take a picture with a camera the photograph tells you what is there at that moment. The photograph does not tell you what it would be like 'if' the sun were to come out, if the man were thinner, if the boy were to smile, if the woman wore a green dress, etc. In the same way the flowscape is a 'picture' of perception at any one moment. Where there is an interest in an 'if' or possible context change then do another flowscape for that other context.

CREATING CONTEXTS

Quite often there are specific context conditions: war conditions, the context of intense jealousy, if the sun is shining, if he is rich, etc. These are definable contexts. Most of the time, however, a context is not defined but is built up of many different factors: experience, prejudice, culture, the media, etc.

At the beginning of the book I mentioned that one characteristic of water is that you could add water to water and still get just water – in contrast to adding rock to rock. So we can build up contexts in layers.

We add further inputs one after the other. The inputs do not have to be connected. The inputs may be contradictory. We just add them. Gradually a context builds up. Poetry and much of art is concerned with the build up of a mood, scene or understanding in this way. There is no attempt to interconnect the elements or to make deductions: the mood just develops.

In the creative process, people are often asked to saturate their minds with information and considerations about the subject and then to let these settle down on their own.

In the book *I am Right – You are Wrong* the process is formalized as a 'stratal'. This is different layers or strata which have no connexion other than that they are about the same subject and are put down in the same place. The result is very similar to blank verse or even a Japanese haiku. There is no conclusion and there is no intention to make any point.

All this is sensible and reasonable behaviour in a self-organizing system. The inputs do organize themselves to give an output which we might call intuition. More importantly we build up a background context in which our thinking can take place.

In setting out to create a flowscape it can be worthwhile to establish the context in this way: putting down layers of statements and considerations. This creates the context in which the flowscape is going to be set. From this also comes the stream of consciousness list of points. This preliminary stage is a sort of sensitizing of the mind to the subject.

ACCURACY AND VALUE

If flow and water logic are so heavily dependent on context and if context can be so variable, then how can a flowscape ever be accurate or have a value? Our actions arise from our perceptions and we do manage to initiate and carry through sensible actions. Perceptions are changeable but are also stable enough to give us actions and flowscapes. If I asked you to arrange the numbers 3 5 2 4

1 6 from the smallest to the biggest, you would have little difficulty in putting down 1 2 3 4 5 6. If I asked you to arrange the numbers 2 13 8 20 3 9 from the smallest to the biggest, you would not tell me that it is impossible because all the numbers are not there. You would arrange them quite simply: 2 3 8 9 13 20. In the same way a flowscape does not have to be comprehensive to have value. We arrange what we have and then see what we get.

'Accuracy' is a term which comes directly from rock logic. Is the flowscape an accurate reflection of the perception of the person making the flowscape? If it is made honestly then it will be a reflection of that person's perception – because it is made with perception. If the person puts down what he or she 'thinks they ought to think' then that is the picture that will emerge.

The value of a flowscape is that it allows us to look at our perceptions. We can agree with them or disagree with them. We may get insights and also a sense of relative importance and controlling factors. We may observe how the perceptions might be changed. We may get ideas or approaches for acting in the outer world represented by the flowscape of the inner world. All these things are values. Could we end up fooling ourselves? The answer is certainly 'yes' because we are very good at that. But we have a much better chance of detecting the self-deception with a flowscape than without it.

Flowscapes do not have a 'proving value' as in rock logic. Their value is illustrative and suggestive. A flow-scape provides a framework or hypothesis for looking at the world. A flowscape provides a tangible way of getting to work on our perceptions.

Do not set out to construct the 'correct' flowscape. Put down the stream of consciousness list and then work forward from that and see what emerges. Then look at that.

FLOWSCAPES FOR OTHER PEOPLE

Flowscapes are primarily intended for yourself, to reflect the water logic and flow of a personal perception. When carried out for yourself a flowscape is tentative, provisional and suggestive. When a flowscape is carried out for someone else, it can only be speculative. It is very difficult to get to know someone else's perceptions even if that person wishes to reveal them.

We can look at three situations in which an attempt might be made to construct a flowscape for someone else:

1. From written, spoken or otherwise expressed material.

2. Guessing.

3. Based on discussion.

FROM WRITTEN MATERIAL ETCETERA

You can listen to a speech, look at a leader in a newspaper, read an article, etc., and then seek to put together a flowscape based on that. The key question is whether the flowscape is your perception of what is expressed or the perception of the writer or speaker. Both are valid, both are possible. It is useful to be clear which one is being attempted. The two may be close together if the writing is clear and the subject is not controversial.

Consider the following passage about the effect of small businesses on employment: 'Small businesses are likely to provide the greatest increase in employment. Big businesses cut down staff with efficiency drives, and also replace them with automation and more and more productive machinery. A small business that takes on three more people may be doubling its workforce. Major businesses never double their work force. Small businesses are into niche markets and services. If there is money to pay for it there will always be a need for more and more service: entertainment; doing your shopping for you; doing your tax for you; health care; etc. Small businesses can start up very quickly. It is very rare to start up a big business. Small businesses have to be risk takers because the entrepreneurs who start them are working on inspiration, hunch, aggression and stupidity. They take risks which a calculating big business with shareholders could never take.

'That is why we should do more to encourage and look after small business. Does this mean that we should keep alive small businesses that fail? No, but we should make it easier for businesses to succeed by removing burdens. We should also make it more attractive for people to start up small businesses.'

LIST

A   INCREASE IN EMPLOYMENT   G

B   ENTREPRENEURS ABLE TO TAKE
    RISKS   D

C   NICHE-SEEKING   J

D   EASE/DIFFICULTY OF START-UP   A

E   SERVICE GROWTH   D

F   MOTIVATION TO START   D

G   REMOVE BURDENS, MAKE IT EASIER TO
    SUCCEED   F

H   BIG BUSINESS TENDS TO SHED PEOPLE   A

I   PEOPLE-INTENSIVE   A

J   SMALL BUSINESSES GROW   A

It may be wondered why H, BIG BUSINESS TENDS TO SHED PEOPLE, should be put as flowing to A, INCREASE IN EMPLOYMENT. This seems a contradiction. Remember, however, that flow is not cause and effect. Because big business tends to shed people we think of an increase in employment as having to come from small business. You might also take it as: since big business tends to shed people, how are we going to increase employment? Both examples lead to the flow chosen.

FLOWSCAPE

The flowscape is shown in fig. 73.

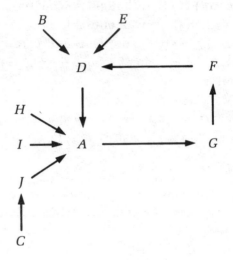

Fig. 73

Point D
This is a collector point relating to the ease of starting up a small business. It covers two aspects: that it is easy to start up a small business and that it should be made easy.

Point A
This collector point covers both an increase in employment and, implicitly, a desired decrease in unemployment. This is fed by a number of factors as indicated.

Loop D–A–G–F

The loop really starts at *G*. Making it easier to succeed leads to increased motivation to start up which helps the ease of starting up a small business. This leads to an increase in employment which is the reason for making it easier for small businesses to succeed.

It may be noted that although the 'action suggestions' part of the written piece was only a fraction of the whole, this part forms the stabilizing loop and core of the flowscape. This is not surprising because the rest is description and explanation.

In this particular case the flowscape is easy and it is likely that this flowscape represents the perception of the author of the piece.

In examining any written, or spoken, piece it is important to separate out the important concepts from mere descriptive lists. Very often the descriptive lists can be covered by a single concept. Skill in the use and description of concepts is crucial. It is simply not feasible to put every feature on the flowscape, so powerful concepts need to be used to cover aspects of the perception.

It is worth repeating the exercise with different connecting flows to see what it looks like. You can then choose which flowscape seems best to reflect the point of the material.

GUESSING

Very often we have to guess at the perceptions of another party. Suppose we go back to the problem used earlier of the neighbour who plays music too loudly at night. We laid out a flowscape from the point of view of the sufferer. We could now try to guess at the perception of the neighbour who is playing the music.

LIST

A   COMPLAINER IS TOO FUSSY   F

B   PLAYING MUSIC IS NORMAL
     BEHAVIOUR   E

C   HATES BEING RESTRICTED AND TOLD
     WHAT TO DO   H

D   COMPLAINER IS JUST BEING SILLY   F

E   NOTHING THE COMPLAINER CAN DO   F

F   HE WILL GET USED TO IT
     EVENTUALLY   G

G   NOT GOING TO GIVE WAY   F

H   ENJOYS THE FIGHT   *G*

I   NO ONE ELSE IS COMPLAINING   *A*

J   LIKES LOUD MUSIC   *B*

There is no way of checking this out. It is just speculation. Nevertheless, there are reasonable guesses and unrea-
sonable ones. It is fair in this sort of situation to put
down the harsher or more extreme possibilities – as a sort
of worst case scenario.

FLOWSCAPE

The flowscape is shown in fig. 74.

Point F

This is a classic collector point which drains the entire
field. It summarizes the situation: the neighbour believes
that the complainer will eventually get used to it and stop
complaining. From this basis the sufferer could put together a strategy of gradually escalating the complaints
(increasing the frequency of phone calls) to indicate that
he or she is not getting used to the noise.

This perception may, in fact be incorrect. The music
player may not care whether the complainer gets used to
it or not. The music player may consider it normal behaviour to which he has every right. In this case the flow
connectors might be different.

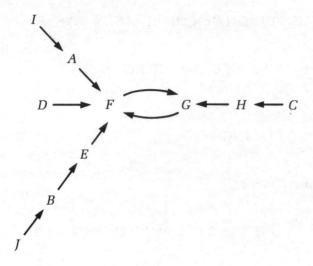

Fig. 74

NEW LIST

A   COMPLAINER IS TOO FUSSY   B

B   PLAYING MUSIC IS NORMAL
     BEHAVIOUR   C

C   HATES BEING RESTRICTED AND TOLD
     WHAT TO DO   G

D   COMPLAINER IS JUST BEING SILLY   B

E   NOTHING THE COMPLAINER CAN DO   B

F   HE WILL GET USED TO IT
     EVENTUALLY   H

G   NOT GOING TO GIVE WAY   C

H   ENJOYS THE FIGHT   G

I   NO ONE ELSE IS COMPLAINING   B

J   LIKES LOUD MUSIC   I

FLOWSCAPE

The new flowscape is shown in fig. 75.

Point B
The collector point is now different. The neighbour believes playing music to be quite normal and within his rights.

Loop C–G
The neighbour does not like being restricted and told what to do, so he is not going to give way.

    This is a much more difficult situation and may have to depend on some objective measurement and a legal move.

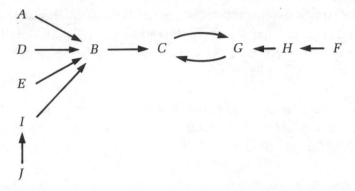

Fig. 75

Since the second guess turns out to be so different from the first, how do we know which is the more correct? There is no easy way of telling. It might make sense to pursue both strategies at once: increase the complaints and also obtain some objective measurement. In any case, the objective measurement will give more force to the complaints and will also show that the sufferer is not going to get used to it. As is usually the case in water logic, the pragmatic or flow view prevails. What does this course of action lead to?

DISCUSSION

Here it is assumed that the other party is cooperating in the construction of the flowscape. This also applies to a group discussion in which the intention is to put forward a joint or group flowscape. Because perception is so individual there is something unsatisfactory about a group or 'average' flowscape. It might be better for the members of the group to construct their own individual flowscapes and then to compare them. Nevertheless, it is possible to construct a group flowscape. The following sequence of steps would be followed.

We must assume that the process has been explained to the group, who understand what is meant by the stream of consciousness list.

1. Construct the stream of consciousness or base list. This can be done with individual suggestions that are added to a visible master list on a board or flip chart. More points than are needed are put down. These points are then reduced by combining points under a single concept or choosing only the more significant points. Another way to do it is to ask for base lists from each person and then to combine these into a master list.

2. Flow connexions are suggested for each point. Sometimes it can be better to start with the more obvious ones on which there is likely to be agreement. Where there is firm disagreement, then the different flow connexions are recorded so that they can be tried out later. It may be necessary to change the concept, or the concept description, on the base list in order to get agreement on the flow connexions.

3. Lay out the flowscape. Where there has not been agreement on the connexions, then different flowscapes are made to show the different possibilities. The different choice of connexions may or may not make much difference to the eventual flowscape.

4. Examine and comment upon the flowscape. Various interventions may be suggested by the group members.

It is important that the flowscape should reflect the genuine perceptions of the individuals in the group. It should not just be a matter of what they believe they should think. It is also important to explain that the flowscape is not an analysis of the situation. Nor is the flowscape a system diagram of what may be happening in the outer world. The flowscape is a flow organization of a perceptual stream of consciousness.

The main value of the group exercise is to explore differences of perception in the setting up stage and then to have something tangible to look at and comment upon when the flowscape is completed. The discussion itself is probably the most important aspect.

HYPOTHESIS

If setting out a flowscape for someone else is so much of a guess, is it worth doing? A hypothesis is also a reasonable guess and yet has proved very useful in allowing us to devise tests of the hypothesis. The 'guessed' flowscape allows us to see which points need focusing upon and checking out. A guess does not prove anything but does tell us where to look for proof. In constructing a flowscape for someone else, it is better not to infer perceptions from actions. So many different perceptions can lead to the same action that it is easy to be misled.

It is better to construct the flowscape from the total situation and then see whether the actions fit that flowscape.

In negotiating, bargaining and conflict situations each party is always trying to figure out the thinking of the other party. This is usually done in a piecemeal way. The flowscape is a way of putting it all together so that we can see the 'shape' of the thinking of the other party.

Politicians, advertisers and market analysts depend very much on assessing the perceptions of the public. Polls will give a good indication, which is improved when key questions can be asked. The flowscape can be a help in determining what the key questions might be.

In all, our own perceptions and the perceptions of others are of great importance. Outside strictly technical matters, perception is often more important than reality.

ATTENTION FLOW

You are walking through long grass and suddenly you hear a rustle right behind you. Your attention switches to that rustle. You are examining a piece of jewellery and the assistant puts another piece in front of you. Your attention switches to the new piece. You are talking to someone at a cocktail party and suddenly one of her earrings falls off. Your attention switches to that. It is hardly surprising that if something new turns up your attention may be caught by that. But what about those situations where there is nothing new? How then does attention shift or flow?

You can live in a house for years and not notice some feature until a guest points it out. The Boy Scouts have a game, called, I believe, Kim's Game, in which you are presented with a tray of objects which is then removed after a few moments. You try to recall as many objects as you can. Noticing things is certainly not easy and may require a lot of training. Medical students are taught to notice all sorts of features of a patient in order to help with the diagnosis. Conan Doyle applied his medical training in this respect to the behaviour of his detective character, Sherlock Holmes.

There is a sort of paradox in that the mind is extremely good at recognizing things and yet poor at noticing things. From a tiny fraction of a familiar picture someone will recognize the picture. From a single bar someone will recognize a musical piece. Perhaps there is no paradox at all. We notice the familiar things we are prepared to notice. At the same time very unusual things will catch our attention. Anything in between is unlikely to be noticed. This is not at all a bad design for a living creature to make its way through life.

In many amusement parks today there are long water chutes in which a little water running down a chute provides enough slipperiness for a child to slide down the entire chute. The surface has to be very smooth. Imagine the trouble that would be caused by a protruding bolt. There is the same effect when something interferes with the smooth flow of attention.

The opposite of interruption is the smooth flow that contributes to aesthetics. In a way art is a choreography of attention, leading attention first here and then there. The same is true of the art of a good storyteller. There is background and foreground and loops of attention. You look at a beautiful Georgian house set amongst trees. At first you look at the whole setting. Then your attention moves to the house itself. Then to the portico or main door. Then back to the house. Then to an individual window. It is this dance of attention that gives us the feeling of pleasure. It is probably true that there are certain things that the human mind finds intrinsically attractive. There are certain proportions which may or may not reflect the proportions of a mother's face to an infant. There are certain rhythms which may or may not be related to the effect of the mother's heartbeat upon a child. The rest may be the rhythm of the flow of attention. In a sense all art is a sort of music.

We often think of attention as a person holding a torch and directing the beam at one thing after another. This does happen sometimes. If you attend very formal art appreciation classes you may be given a sort of check-list of attention. Notice the use of light and shade. Notice the disposition of the figures. Notice the use of colour. Notice the brushwork. Notice the faces, etc. Here, attention is flowing along a pre-set pattern in order to notice things in the world in front.

Mostly, however, there are no check-lists except those set by familiarity and expectation. Mostly attention flows according to the rules of water logic. If the flow of attention turns up something interesting then there is a new direction, and new loops form. You might be looking at the carving on a Hindu temple and suddenly notice a swastika sign. Because of the association of the swastika with Nazi Germany your attention is caught and loops around in that area. You may wonder what the sign is doing there if you do not know that it is indeed an ancient Hindu symbol.

So the attention flow itself can turn up things which develop further attention flows. You are looking at something in a museum and then you read the label – this prompts you to notice things you have not noticed. So even if there are no new events, attention can turn up 'new events'.

If attention follows the rules of water logic then why does attention not lock itself into a stable pattern and stay there? To some extent this is what attention normally does. Most of the time we recognize things and do not give them a second glance, precisely because we have locked into the usual stable pattern. At other times the flow of attention uncovers new things which then develop new loops. Any new input will change the context and so get us out of a stabilized loop.

Attention flow may uncover areas of richness and detail. The immense richness of the carvings on a Hindu temple makes it difficult for us to see it as a whole. In contrast, the attention flow of the Taj Mahal is an excellent example of a smooth flow from the whole to a part and back to the whole and back to another part, and so on. If there is too much detail we get bogged down. If there is too little detail we can only see the whole, and attention does not flow – as in some modern buildings. Somewhere between too much and too little detail is the richness of the Gothic style. This is more like the intricacies of a morris dance rather than the waltz of the classical style, although that could also have many intricacies.

The difference between perception which is purely internal and attention flow which is directed outwards is that attention can trigger new perceptions. This can also happen in the inner world of reflective perception but is much more rare. In general, in reflective perception, it is a matter of existing perceptions which organize themselves into flow patterns which we attempt to capture with flowscapes.

If a dog is taken on a walk then the dog will stop, sniff around and explore one area then set off for another area, which is then explored again, and so on. Attention flow is somewhat like that. Fig. 76 shows that the overall track of

attention flow is really made up of several exploratory
loops on the way.

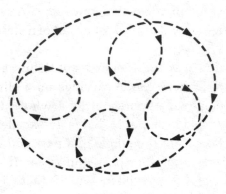

Fig. 76

If we include the loops in the overall track then fig. 77
shows some possible attention-flow tracks. In one case
the track just wanders about. In another case the track
keeps coming back to the starting point but then moves
out in widening circles, all of which still come back to the
start. In another case the loops succeed each other but the
whole returns full circle to the starting point. I suspect the
attention flows that complete the circles are the ones
which we would find most appealing.

'ISNESS'

Indian philosophies put a lot of emphasis on 'isness'
which means really seeing what something 'is'. If you sit
and contemplate a rose for three hours you will begin to

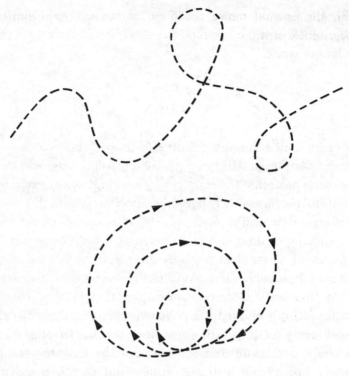

Fig. 77

see a 'rose'. Mostly attention has a practical job to do: explore a matter until you recognize it and then move on. Once the perceptual loop has stabilized we move on. So we do not really see a rose but just the usual impression of a rose.

Meditation is an attempt to halt the flow of attention and to unravel the stable perceptual loops. One can ascribe metaphysical value to that as you wish. A somewhat similar effect can be obtained with drugs that interfere with the normal nerve coordination, so making familiar things look strange because the established flow patterns no longer work.

TENSION

Salvador Dali's famous painting of the melting watch is a pure example of the use of the tension between two opposing patterns: the rigidity of a watch that is necessary for it to perform its function of accuracy, and the soft contours of wax-like melting. The mixing, opposing and juxtaposing of images has an extensive tradition in art. It is unusual, it catches our attention and makes us stop, think and perceive anew. Without claiming that it is easy to do this well, it can be said that this is a relatively simple technique used also by bad artists and bad poets to achieve effect. To talk about the 'cold fire of his spirit' creates a perceptual tension between the normal perception of fire as hot and the attachment of the image of 'cold'. The mind does not quite know how to settle down and oscillates between the two images, creating an effect more powerful than 'the fire of his spirit'. There is genuine descriptive value in that the 'cold fire' does suggest a passion that is cold, calculating and ruthless.

A significant part of art is based on the need to unsettle the usual. Normally attention does its work and moves on. Attention flow is normally dismissive. Art seeks to highlight, to deepen perception and to open up insights. This is done by disrupting patterns, by juxtaposing patterns, by providing new pattern frameworks.

If attention were a cook it would always contentedly cook the same dishes. By interfering with the cooking, by providing new ingredients, by removing staple ingredients, art sets out to re-excite our taste buds with new dishes that allow us to taste the old ingredients anew.

When the Impressionists first started to show their work it was judged hideous and ugly by most of the art critics and connoisseurs. This was because it was 'ugly' when viewed through the frames of expectation of existing and traditional painting. People had to be trained to look at the paintings in a different way to appreciate their beauty. Carrying this to an extreme, if you put a pile of bricks into an art gallery and you ask people to look at the bricks as a work of art then they really do become a work of art. This circles back to the 'isness' I mentioned before. Our normal perception patterns treat bricks as mundane building materials but if we break that loop we see them differently but still keep a faint echo of their constructive value.

TRIGGERING

A finger on a trigger can release a child's pop gun or a nuclear bomb. There is no direct relationship between the pressure on the trigger and the effect. A system is set 'to go' and you trigger it to go. Perception has already set up the patterns which are ready to go. The triggers or stimulation we receive from the world around set off flow patterns in the brain which settle down into the standard perception. It is something like those children's play books in which the child is asked to join up the given dots.

The patterns that we operate as perception depend upon the triggers received, past experience and the organizing behaviour of the brain. It is this organizing behaviour that has been the subject of this book. This behaviour involves the formation of temporarily stable states which tire and are succeeded by other similar states in the flow of water logic. This flow itself stabilizes as a loop and that forms the standard perception.

Attention flow is determined by the outer world and also by the standard perception patterns which direct where we should look in order to check out the suitability of the patterns. It is very similar to a conversation. In a conversation you listen to what is being said but your own mind is going about its own business. So we pay attention to what is out there but our own brain is busy with its perception patterns and flows. Just as the leaves of a tree all 'flow' down the branches into the tree trunk so the different sensations are 'drained' into an established flow pattern.

DIRECTING ATTENTION

Attention flow is determined by what is out there, by our standard perceptual patterns, by the context of the moment and what we may be trying to do. Is this natural flow of attention the most beneficial or effective? It may be effective for long-term survival of the species: do not waste energy on what you already know and what is not valuable at the moment. But it is less than effective for other matters. The whole purpose of a university education is supposed to be to train the mind to probe more deeply–and this requires attention-directing practice. The formal check-list for art appreciation that I gave earlier is a simple example of attention directing. It may seem rigid and mechanical but in time it does result in better attention flows.

The very first lesson in the CoRT thinking programme for teaching thinking as a school subject has a simple attention-directing device called the PMI. The student directs his or her attention to the Plus aspects of the situation, then the Minus aspects and finally the Interesting aspects. If people do this anyway, as some claim, then the exercise should make no difference. Instead we get huge differences in final judgement (from 30 out of 30 students being in favour of an idea to only one being in favour). There is no mystery. The normal attention flow results in an immediate emotional reaction which then determines an attention flow to support that reaction. The PMI ensures a basic exploration of the subject before judgement. This is not at all natural. What is natural is to interpret, recognize and judge as quickly as possible. That has long-term survival value.

The flowscapes put forward in this book are attention-directing devices in the sense that the examination of a flowscape can direct our attention to the significant parts of our own perception.

DIFFICULTIES

In using the flowscape technique, what are the difficulties likely to be?

The first difficulty is likely to be an inadequate base list. This may truly be inadequate or you may feel it to be inadequate. You may feel that there is something inexact about a stream of consciousness list which is so different from a careful analysis. There is no need at all to feel this for reasons I have gone into before. There is the 'hologram effect' which just means that in perception each aspect reflects something of the whole. The other reason is that water logic is different from rock logic. Adding some more leaves to a tree does not make much difference to the structure of that tree.

Your base list may indeed be inadequate in the sense that you have on the list too many details and too few concepts. Concepts are powerful because they cover many things. If you find you tend to have too many details, go through the list and attempt to replace details with a broader concept. For example instead of 'shoes' you might put the broader concept 'clothes' and even the broader concept 'material needs'. The other thing to do is to make a much longer list and then go through it, reducing the number by combining some of the items on the list. Normally it is quite hard to generate even ten good points for the base list and twenty is really difficult. If, on the contrary, you find it easy to generate the points then keep going until you run out. Then go back and reduce the list.

It does take some practice to get a useful base list. It is like the practice required to ride a bicycle. It is awkward rather than difficult and if you keep going you will suddenly get the knack of it.

The next possible difficulty is in setting up the flow connexions between the points on the base list. This can be a genuine difficulty because our minds are more full of 'cause and effect' than of 'flow'. There are two possible types of difficulty. An item on the base list just does not seem to flow into any other item on the list. Or there are so many possible flow connexions for an item that it is difficult – and may seem arbitrary – to select one of them.

If there does not seem to be any obvious connexion then try to look at things in different ways: which of the points comes naturally to mind after this one? In what area does this point lie – is there another point in this area? What follows on from this point? Is there a missing or 'silent' link point which would make the connexion easier?

In the end you have to do your best. Of all the unlikely points on the list, which is the least unlikely? For which point can you make some case for the connexion?

In cases where there seem to be too many possible connexions there are some general rules to follow. As far as possible avoid connecting back to a point from which the connexion has come. For example if you have connected A to H try to avoid connecting H to A. Sometimes this is inevitable and necessary but on the whole it is too easy just to reverse a connexion and too easy to form a stable loop this way. Do not just choose the broadest concept because that is easiest. Make an effort to select the strongest connexion rather than the easiest. By strongest I mean the one which follows more powerfully.

If you still have serious doubts, then try out two or more flowscapes with your different choices of perception.

We can try a simple example to illustrate some of these points.

SUBJECT

Someone is thinking about looking around for a new job. This person has not been approached with an offer of a new job but is thinking of looking around.

LIST

A   BORED

B   BETTER PROSPECTS

C   NEED A CHANGE

D   NEW PEOPLE

E   BETTER SALARY

F   START AFRESH

G   CHANGE IMAGE

H   BETTER LOCATION

I   HASSLE/BOTHER OF CHANGE

J   UNCERTAINTY OF CHANGE

We start with *A*, BORED, and this seems to connect directly with *C*, NEED A CHANGE. It could possibly also lead to *D*, NEW PEOPLE, or *F*, START AFRESH, if the person laying out the flowscape did have a particular concern with the people in the present job or the present image. This would be a personal matter which would affect the connexion.

B, BETTER PROSPECTS, leads directly to *E*, BETTER SALARY. In a sense a better salary is part of better prospects.

The item *C*, NEED A CHANGE, is more difficult because it could just lead straight back to *A*, BORED. We could connect up with *F*, START AFRESH. We might also connect up with *I*, HASSLE/BOTHER OF CHANGE, in the sense that any change involves hassle and bother. We choose *F*, START AFRESH.

D, NEW PEOPLE could lead to *F*, START AFRESH or *A*, BORED, depending on the person making the flowscape. If there were difficulties with the present people then *F*, START AFRESH, would be more relevant. Otherwise the choice is for *A*, BORED.

E, BETTER SALARY, could very easily link back to B, BETTER PROSPECTS since the two are almost synonymous. Instead we choose H, BETTER LOCATION. This may seem odd. The reasoning is that both better salary and better location are reasons for wanting to change. The connexion is an 'and' type of connexion. The mind flows that way.

F, START AFRESH, is connected up with G, CHANGE IMAGE. It could just as well have been connected with D, NEW PEOPLE, if, in an individual case, existing people were a problem, or boring.

G, CHANGE IMAGE, could feed right back into F, START AFRESH, but connects more strongly to C, NEED A CHANGE.

H, BETTER LOCATION, connects up with B, BETTER PROSPECTS, as it is one type of better prospect and an improved quality of life. The notion of 'quality of life' is a silent link here.

I, HASSLE/BOTHER OF CHANGE, leads on to J, UNCERTAINTY OF CHANGE, better than to anything else as both are the negatives of the matter.

J, UNCERTAINTY OF CHANGE, leads back to I, HASSLE/BOTHER OF CHANGE.

FLOWSCAPE

The flowscape is shown in fig. 78. Interestingly the flowscape has separated out into three stable loops.

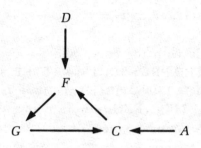

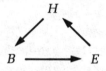

Fig. 78

Loop C–F–G

This loop covers the negative reasons for wanting to change. That is to say the reasons why the present state of affairs is not satisfactory: NEED A CHANGE, START AFRESH, CHANGE IMAGE. Another negative factor feeding it is boredom. The NEW PEOPLE factor is negative if the present people are difficult or boring, but might otherwise be regarded as a positive factor. This depends, as in all flowscapes, on individual situations and perception.

Loop B–E–H

The loop deals with the hopes and positive aspect of a change: BETTER PROSPECTS, BETTER SALARY and BETTER LOCATION. These are things that can be looked foward to. It could be argued that if the present salary, prospects and location are actually bad, these are also negative factors. But at least they refer to the new situation rather than the old one.

Loop I–J

This simple loop puts together HASSLE/BOTHER OF CHANGE and UNCERTAINTY OF CHANGE. It seems appropriate that these should be in their own loop because they really are independent of the reasons for wanting to change. The decision to change does not need to be separated from the difficulties of making the change otherwise these factors play too large a part in the decision.

This flowscape does seem an acceptable version of the perceptions involved. In an individual case the connexions and the flowscape might look different. For example a difficult boss might be a reason for wanting to change. Lack of people of marriageable age might also be another reason since so many people marry those they work with. Perceptions are always individual. In individual cases the connexions are much easier than in abstract or general cases since the contexts are so much more specific. Whenever you look at a flowscape put together by someone else, all you can say is: 'I would have made different connexions.' You cannot tell the other person that his or her flowscape is wrong just because you see things differently.

ERRORS

Can there be misleading errors in a flowscape? Since a flowscape does not claim to be right it is difficult for it to be wrong. A flowscape is a hypothesis or a suggestion. It is a provisional way of looking at the shape of our perceptions. If we do not like what we see then we can check out what it is that we do not like. When we get a surprise, we may find it is the surprise of insight: 'I did not realize that point was as central as it is.'

Since most of the attention is on collector points and stable loops, there is a danger that an important point which just happens to feed into a collector point will not get the attention it deserves. In a way this is as it should be because collector points and loops do dominate perception. We usually believe that important points should dominate perception but very often they do not. A flowscape is a picture of perception as it is, not as it should be.

There is a danger of constructing a false flowscape, which is one which is carefully contrived to give you the perception you think you ought to have. In such cases you are cheating no one but yourself. There is no limit to the number of flowscapes you can lay out on any subject. You may vary the connexions and make another flowscape. You can alter some of the items on the base list and make a further flowscape. Examine them all and see what you can get from them.

When you attempt to make flowscapes for other people you may be totally in error. You have to keep that in mind. Your perception of another person's perception may leave out something vital. If the perception can be checked out in some way then that should be done. If not, then design strategies which fit various possibilities. Or just accept the risk that you may have got it wrong and go ahead with your strategy, but be prepared to change the strategy if it does not seem to be working.

SUMMARY

Our traditional rock logic is based on 'is' which leads us on to 'identity', 'truth', 'contradiction' and 'logic'. Mathematics is based on the 'equals' sign which allows us to operate the rules of the game of the mathematical universe. Water logic is based on 'to' and the concept of 'flow'. In certain systems flow leads to 'stable loops'. A stable loop is not the same as 'truth' – it is a stable loop which we can learn to use just as we learned to use truth.

Fig. 79 shows the symbolic difference between the three systems of rock logic, mathematics and water logic. This is obviously an oversimplification but it does make the difference clear.

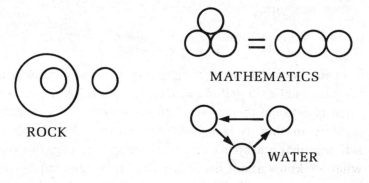

Fig. 79

It is actually very difficult for us to think in terms of water logic because language itself and our habits of thinking are so thoroughly based on rock logic. We can just about be concerned with pragmatism and what things lead 'to' but our reasoning is still based on rock logic, and we keep coming back to it with such remarks as, 'Is this right?'

As I wrote at the beginning, the book is actually very simple. I have tried to keep it simple in order to provide a practical introduction to water logic. I have wanted to provide a method that people can use for themselves instead of just reading about it. There is far more to water logic than I have covered in this book but I have not wanted to deter readers with complexity. I hope to be able to take the matter further in later works.

There are two base theorems, both of which are simple:

1. In any system with a finite number of states and a tiring factor, a stable loop will always be established from any input.

2. Under a given context X, A will always lead to B.

In the book, I have examined how the nerve circuits in the brain act as a self-organizing system to allow perceptions to arrange themselves into stable states. There is no mystery in this. It is simple, fundamental behaviour of self-organizing systems and well within the capability of what we know about nerve circuits. Although simple, this behaviour is extremely powerful. I explore this behaviour in more detail in another book, *I am Right — You are Wrong*, to which I have made reference as appropriate. This sort of thinking is now mainstream thinking amongst many working on brain behaviour — although it was far from mainstream when I wrote about it in 1969 in *The Mechanism of Mind*.

I am not interested in merely analysing and describing the behaviour of the brain, nor am I especially interested in designing computers that think like the brain does. But I am interested in ways of improving human thinking.

So there is a practical side to the book. This practical side is the flowscape. This technique is described in detail with many examples.

The laying out of a flowscape is very straightforward. There is the stream of consciousness or base list. Flow connexions are made for each item on the base list. The result is displayed graphically. We can now get to see the 'shape' of our perceptions.

Perceptions are highly individual, so there is no matter of saying this is right or wrong, unless you are guessing at the perception of some other person. The flowscape is a hypothesis which we look at in order to examine our perceptions. From such an examination we may come to see the collector points or sinks which draw other points towards them. Such collector points tend to dominate any perception. Then there are the stable loops which stabilize perceptions.

We may get some understanding of our perception and even some insights into what is going on. We may come to realize that some points are more important and others less important than we thought.

We can try to intervene and see how our perceptions might be altered. Although we are intervening in the inner world of perception we can get suggestions that may also be useful for intervening in the outer world. So we can devise strategies based on flowscapes. Such strategies are suggested by the flowscape but must be proved in other ways. This is the same as with any hypothesis.

We can set out to make flowscapes for other people. This can be done through discussion as with a group. It can also be done by examining the writing or utterances of the other person. Finally we can attempt to make a flowscape for another person by guessing. Such flowscapes can suggest strategies and actions.

In the book I write about the huge importance of concepts for water logic. It is concepts that give movement and flexibility in thinking. Such concepts do not always need to be precise because we are using water logic rather than rock logic, which depends on precision. If we do not develop a facility for dealing with concepts then we are locked into the literal details of experience. Concepts are also important for the base list of the flowscape.

Context is hugely important in the flow of water logic. If the context is different then the flow connexions are different. Any indication of flow should always specify the context. Although context is so very important this does not complicate the flowscape provided this is done at one moment in time. The context of that moment will affect the whole flowscape, which becomes a picture of perception at that moment. Most disagreements are really based on differences of context. Yet we usually direct our thinking to arguing about differences of 'truth'.

Towards the end of the book I write about attention flow and also its relevance to aesthetics and art. Attention flow is partly determined by what is out there, partly by the perceptual patterns of our inner world and partly by specific attention-directing patterns that we have developed deliberately. There is a close connexion between perceptual patterns and attention flow. The world outside triggers the patterns that we then use to 'see' the world outside. Like much else this matter deserves much fuller attention.

I have set out to achieve three things:

1. An introduction to water logic.

2. An explanation of how the water logic of perception is based on the self-organizing nature of the nerve circuits in the brain.

3. A practical technique to make visible the flow patterns of our perception so that we can see the 'shape' of our thinking. This is the flowscape technique.

The flowscape technique can be used in its own right even if you do not accept, or understand, the basis for it.

The purpose of any conceptual model is to provide something useful and usable. That itself is an example of water
logic: 'What does this lead to?'

I am aware that the rigidities of rock logic will make
some people uncomfortable with this book. At the same
time there are many who will welcome the fluidity of
water logic because such people have always felt that
rock logic is totally inappropriate and inadequate to deal
with perceptions. And perceptions are extremely important.